Halcyon Haze

Mimi Cox

Available at: www.createspace.com/3607846,
Amazon.com, and other retailers
Further contacts,halcyon.haze@yahoo.com

ISBN: 0615509479
ISBN-13: 9780615509471

❦

This book is dedicated to Steve and his chickens.

❦

❧

This work is a memoir. It reflects the author's present recollection of her experiences over a period of years. Certain names and identifying characteristics have been changed.

❧

I would like to give my heart felt thanks to Max Load for giving me permission to use his poems, songs and drawings. But most important, I would like to thank him for allowing my authentic self to sparkle.

CHAPTER ONE

"Get It While You Can"
Janis Joplin

Lying on a cot at her parent's summer cottage in southern Ontario, Mimi squeezed her eyes shut as she rubbed her legs, allowing the grains of sand to create a sensation not unlike sandpaper and giving urgency to the start of a new day. Mimi was restless that morning. She jumped out of bed and kicked off her Tweety bird slippers and pulled up her knee-high suede boots. She was unaware that the first steps of a journey away from her sheltered childhood, Detroit-suburbia world would soon take place. Named after her oldest sister's doll, Mimi was a teenage Catholic girl ready to begin her freshman year at Rosary High in the fall of 1968. Up to that time, Mimi felt as mechanical and lifeless as her sister's doll, opening toy-like eyes onto a safe and too predictable future.

"The all-girl high school was just boring enough that I could revel in daydreams and still pay enough attention to get good grades. Images of gloomy Detroit side streets and back-alley dangers floated freely in and out of my studies, with the drone of the teacher's voice in the background. I began wondering what it was like to live among the factories and smoky side streets that encased the disappointed lives, failed plans, and doomed romances; to live among a gathering place of decapitated, rubber doll heads lying next to trash cans on the curbs of brown, dead lawns."

A different kind of Oz.
No rules,
Payday Fridays and
Bed-spring romances.

"As the freight trains clanked past on the inner city-bound rails that ran beside my history class window, I could easily get sidetracked fantasizing about the characters that lived in the slums of Detroit. There would be a few times that my dad would honor my request to drive through the parts of town where the poor people lived just as we crossed over the Ambassador Bridge from Canada. I had a fascination for the city's rawness that exposed the steel power from its sweaty industrial muscle, just as I was equally captivated by the natural strengths of its girls working the street corner.

"It was at this time, when I started to frequent secondhand stores, that I began to look for the kaleidoscope of cast-off clothes that would be a basis for a sense of fashion expressing my individuality. My unconventional taste made the old new again. My classmates thought my granny shoes and Garbo style strange, indeed.

"Changing the way I dressed was the first rebellious stance I took to outwardly express how I was feeling inwardly. I felt I could no longer follow a blueprint of a generation who believed that the color of a person's skin defined how one should be treated. I timidly started challenging my neighbor's old-school prejudiced remarks that blacks were all lazy and the neighborhood would go down in value as soon as a Negro family moved into Dearborn Heights.

"I found the system hypocritical. My older brothers were forced into a human lottery—the draft—that could possibly, in the near future, order the unlucky first picked to firebomb innocent, Hanoi village children. Meanwhile my brothers peacefully genuflected each week as altar boys during Sunday Mass.

"With the guidance of female activists, I formulated my own opinion of the Church's prohibition against pleasing my modest body myself. This in turn exploded orgasmic liberation from my mother's instilled belief that a woman's pleasure was created in the privacy of her own home, making babies."

"Newly armed with passive aggressiveness, I embellished my conventional school uniform with peace signs and handed out *make love, not war* buttons after school. I attended a sit-in of the resistance group that David Harris and his wife, Joan Baez, founded and participated in. This event simply honored Tom Sincavitch, a draft dodger who returned his draft card to the government and subsequently refused induction. I also decided when the time came I would go on the pill. I donned my POW bracelet and bedded down comfortably in the '60s movement."

Instead of baking cupcakes for prom committees or attending school assembly halls whose main topic was lady-like behavior, Mimi had other priorities. She seized the moment, skipping class to get a groove for the unexplored city world that she wondered about while riding on the Metro Detroit bus.

She sat next to girls that her friends called "greasers," their hair was teased into Tammy Wynette hair-dos, and they contentedly popped their gum while they thought up ways to best stand by their men as they clutched their paper sack lunches. Mimi wondered if the jobs they were headed to were any more stimulating than her Latin classes.

According to Mimi's girlfriend, Pam, the girls' daytime jobs were not so stimulating, but their nighttime duties were. The sister of Pam's boyfriend had to drop out of school to support her baby with a job that only an unwed mother would take.

Detroit's steel-gray winter schooldays did not freeze Mimi's restlessness. Ironically she would find her solace and curb her boredom inside the Penguin House at the Detroit Zoo. Cocooned like those birds in their glass snowball wonderland, she identified with the penguins, swimming in flight. If she stopped gliding in the icy water, Mimi asked herself, could she sink as well?

As the weather warmed and the snow melted, her enthusiasm for diversion did not change. Two of her best friends from grade school—a guy named Frankie Lee from whom she received her first kiss and Kathy, another Rosary girl—frequented the primate pavilion with Mimi. They hung out and watched the red-butt monkeys pick Juju Beads from their teeth after Mimi threw the candy to them.

But the adolescent rebellion of skipping school and the innocent pranks at the zoo soon led to more dangerous escapades.

"When my memory serves me well (and it doesn't at times), my first bold act of defiance was hitchhiking home from classes in my first year, second semester."

"Mimi," said Kathy, "I'm not calling my dad to come get us again because we missed the bus. Be at the bus stop at three o'clock—and don't be late!"

"It was probably intentional, but I just couldn't get it together to be on time for that bus. So the times that I missed it, I would stick my thumb out, alone on the corner of Joy and Greenfield, far enough away from the prying eyes of the nuns, and hitch a ride home."

"Thanks for stopping," Mimi said innocently as she slid into the car, unconcerned about the high heel shoe lying on the back seat or the empty whiskey bottle rolling on the floorboards. She asked, "What's your name?"

"Troy," said the man as he puffed away on his Marlboro, revealing rotten, stained teeth. He leaned slightly over to brush Mimi's hair away from her face. Instinctively Mimi slid closer to the door handle.

"If you wanna be a chick on the road," he continued, venturing on with his hands on Mimi's thigh, "then you hafta be ready to do other things."

It would be years before auto industry engineers would invent driver side door locks, allowing a fortunate Mimi to easily jump out of Troy's car at the next traffic light.

Troy's bad luck and his hard-on intentions were shriveling up by the time Mimi reached Michigan Avenue in Dearborn's business district. She thought she might grab a coke at Kresge's or go to one of the new clothing boutiques called head shops that were springing up.

One such head shop was called the Climax Boutique, which was owned by Nikki and his "old lady," Marion. She did not look old to Mimi. When Mimi noticed her for the first time, opening the front door for business, Marion's long flowing skirt and African scarves caught the wind like a child's kite tail.

To emulate Marion's real gold earrings shimmering gypsy style, Mimi dropped a nickel into the bubble gum machine at Dearborn Music so she could bend the cheap metal into the shape of a hoop to wear as a fake pierced earring. Mimi's mother forbade her to get her ears pierced because people might mistake her for a Jew.

Twenty-five years later, Mimi's Jewish business partner would reveal to her that her mother wouldn't let her get her ears pierced because people might mistake her for an Italian Catholic girl.

Mimi and Marion were like two flowers growing in different types of gardens—one formal, the other wild. But both girls were seeking avenues away from the root-bound beds in which they were planted.

"By her request, I told Marion stories from my storybook life. She was fascinated how I sat with my family every night at six and discussed the common daily happenings with them—all held together by the boring fabric of routine. Marion wanted to know where we went on family vacations and how we democratically voted on the choices of which Route 66 hotels we used when we drove out to California. She wanted me to describe in detail how we chose our Christmas tree and the kind of wrapped presents we might find under its branches. I remembered presents, like the Casper the Ghost doll that would say, "Boo" if you pulled its cord.

Reminiscing about my upbringing, I realized it appeared I had it all. But I had already been living this life for fifteen years and was looking for different, stimulating adventures like the ones I heard Marion describe."

As long as they lived at home under their families' restrictions and ruled by the conventional morals their family units were teaching, Kathy and Mimi would never experience the freedom that Marion had. So, as if in a dress rehearsal for the "Prince and the Pauper," the wannabe Marion's instead settled for trying on the bazaar clothing that was brought back from Marion's travels. Together they tried on the imported sun-colored ponchos—orange and yellow from south of the border—that hung on the Climax's racks, as they listened to Van Morrison singing, "Moon Dance."

The girls giggled at the discovery of what stash bags were, marveled at the flashing metal of a cannabis brass buckle, and remained afraid to ask about the wooden East Indian pipes with the water chambers at their bases. They admired themselves in the mirror when they tried on the hip-hugging, bell-bottom Levi's and bought Yardley London makeup that came from Carnaby Street. This made them the first girls at their school to be hip enough to wear lip gloss together with maxi coats and granny glasses.

Mimi felt sorry for Marion even though she wanted to emulate her lifestyle. She was hard to look at because of the adolescent acne pockmarks on her face," Mimi recalls. "But after you looked past her superficial facial flaws, you found a sensitive, warm-hearted, and adventurous soul inside. She was self-conscious about her appearance, which made her an easy target for receiving second-rate respect from second-rate men.

"Nikki proves my point. They were considered a couple and did have fun smoking dope and traveling together but even that came with a kind of pain. Marion loved Nikki for the time and place he was taking up. But it would have been best for her to leave behind the few sterling memories they had shared than to live with the numerous bad times that remained. The mismatched "temperaments of these two were completely opposite from each other. Nikki had a mean streak, believing that the world owed him, while Marion had a sweet nature, thinking that she owed something to the world. Making money by selling clothes to the rich suburban kids like us was the thread that held their relationship together.

"As one entered the store, the fumes from the weed Nikki chain smoked blended with the incense that burned continuously. Marion had a pet parrot in a metal cage that drew me like a magnet. I usually stopped by the boutique every day to visit with the damned bird, making me late for dinner at home. I just couldn't help myself. The animal mesmerized me. It squawked as Marion would talk about her bohemian life, while smiling with her beatific mouth. Her way of life was completely foreign to me but one I wish I had. She had the freedom to live out west in a commune, followed the Grateful Dead band from time to time, and had no obligations to pass any exams.

"As the story goes, Kathy and I stopped by the store as usual to see Marion and her bird after school. Nikki was also there, and he suggested Marian and Kathy get some coffee down the street at Cunningham's while I stayed and helped him go through the new shipment of embroidered dresses from India—the ones with tiny mirrors sewn on them. I held up the muslin dress that I decided to try on and caught a glimpse of my face reflecting in one of the mirrors. The parrot squawked as I passed by, and it was the first time I had ever seen him ruffle his feathers. I started for the dressing room. As I pulled the dress down over my head, Nikki pulled back the curtain and towered over me. His tattooed, needle-pricked arm pinned me against the full-length mirror. His slurred words whispered in my ear.

"Oh baby, you turn me on. At last I got you alone. I can tell you want it. I got a feeling you taste just like cotton candy. Let me lick some…"

"His hands lifted my flimsy dress. I started to panic when I realized that my strength was no match for his lust. I tried my damnedest to pull away, and shouted at him."

"Nikki, you don't want me. Think of Marion!"

His response: "Fuck her."

Nikki leaned against the mirror anticipating his pleasure as he recklessly kissed Mimi's neck and pushed his cold hand between her warm legs, trying to find a way in. A customer bell pierced the silence, interrupting Mimi's terror.

"Anyone here? Yoo-hoo, anyone around?"

Nikki's powerful grip held Mimi's arms captive, while his other hand cupped her mouth so she couldn't call for help.

"Yoo-hoo. Where is everyone?"

The customer's persistence irritated Nikki. He poked his head outside the curtain to answer the lady that he will be there soon allowing Mimi a chance to bite his hand and break free.

"There you are," said the customer as Mimi frantically rushed past her and out the door.

Nikki began screaming at the customer, "Godammit, I told you I was coming!"

"Before he came, I was already gone," Mimi smirked.

CHAPTER TWO

"Cactus Tree"
Joni Mitchell

"There is a timeline in one's life when memory of the past becomes a muddled reality. The chain of events that took place is replaced by gut feelings. Would it add to my story to know the exact date and time when Max and I met? Would my memory change the intense energy and the attraction I instantly felt for him if I could remember what guided me into The Artist, a local music store, when I wasn't even a musician? I think these trivial details would not.

"What you do need to know is this. Before I met Max, my protective upbringing never allowed my inner beauty and longing to show personal self-expression to surface. My loving parents provided everything I needed outwardly, with an environment in which I was comfortable and confident. But inwardly this almost institutional environment prevented me from finding my self-worth. I needed to emerge into a new world, a world I had never known.

"I was beginning to venture out into uncharted waters, exploring and testing the opportunities my safe harbor otherwise denied me. When I walked into The Artist and Max asked me, "Can I help you?" I was unaware that my authentic gut feeling answered his question literally."

Mimi had been checking out new places to hang out and it was on this day that she peeped into the storefront window. She had planned to buy a Wayne State campus newspaper, when a guy with the bluest eyes she had ever seen came up and asked, "Can I help you?" as he butted his Pall Mall out into the ashtray.

Per aspera ad astra.

"D'ya wanna see a guitar?"

Mimi answered as she noticed the half-inch scar that jagged across his upper cheekbone and wondered if she should fear him or take care of him.

"Yes, err…ah, that one." There were rows of guitars pegged to the walls. She hastily pointed at the first one she saw.

Max's eyes met Mimi's, capturing the feeling born in time. Max took down a guitar different from the one Mimi had chosen.

"This is the one you want," he said with a confident smirk.

Mimi wasn't sure what he was referring to: the guitar or himself.

The wisdom of time will teach anyone that a life can change in a single moment—by a certain event, by confirmed truths, or by a special person that highlights one's own potential. Perhaps in Mimi's case, all three happened. It is said that the only change you can experience is the change you choose to make. She spontaneously and graciously accepted this moment and blossomed with an emotional awakening. When her soul met Max's, the direction of her life changed toward where she wanted to go. Marion gave Mimi new insight to another world, but it was Max who gave her the key to enter it. All she had to do was step over the threshold.

❀

Over the weeks that followed, Max showed Mimi around the innards of Detroit that had always fascinated and intrigued her. The numbness she felt from her formal education was replaced with the energized tingling she experienced from the vibes of the FOX Theater. With the electric neon bulbs that pulsating the rhythm of Woodward Avenue and its people, and the scandalous lives of its performers, Mimi found her daydreams materialize on the pavement up to Cadillac's Square.

The city brought to life Mimi's heated imagination, flaring up when she listened to the informal Beat generation schooling that Max gave her. He taught her about the 1940s music scene at the Horseshoe Bar in the heart of Paradise Valley, the El Sino "Bongo Beat" crowd that had an amazing diversity of hipsters, and the time when the Flame topped its marquee with Billie Holiday. She imagined with all her might what it must have been like inside the smoke-filled bars listening to scratchy jukebox records over one scotch, one bourbon, and one beer.

"See that building over there?" Max enthusiastically pointed. "That's where I got to hear Janis Joplin sing."

Mimi was lost in thought, distracted by the still life masterpiece she was formulating in her head. In her mind's eye she saw the Grande Ballroom's fallen bricks that lay randomly in the alleyway and the water-stained curtains shrouding its rotten windowsill where iconic musicians questioned their fate from within the icy snow globe of time.

"Janis who?" Mimi asked, breaking from her reverie.

"That there is the Detroit Public Library. And across the street is the Art Institute where the Mexican artist, Diego Rivera, painted the mural, brushing his socialistic views on the lobby's wall."

"They don't teach that at Rosary High," she commented.

Armed with the confidence and the logistics of bus transfers and stops that she could now manage herself, Mimi knew her request to her dad for permission to drive through the bad parts of town was a thing of the past. Mimi started to ride alone downtown on the Saturdays when Max was working at The Artist.

Coexisting among the bums and thieves that successfully panhandled a buck from Mimi were deserted clothing stores such as Winkleman's, Marianne's, and Moorhead's—all once thriving businesses that dotted the shopping districts where Mimi remembered back-to-school shopping with her mother. She could see firsthand how sad and rundown the buildings had become.

The experience of riding on the same route triggered reminded Mimi of when she was a little girl and downtown was considered "safe." She noticed a toddler sitting on the lap of his mother looking very secure, sucking on his thumb. The thumb was cracked from sucking but apparently still quite satisfying.

Mimi jerked forward when the massive engine roared along Mack Avenue. Her nose was stuffy from the heating vents that not only circulated the much appreciated warm air to her numbed fingers and toes, but also moved the bottled-up, stinking breath of the bums who sat in the back, thawing out from sleeping on the park benches the night before.

Mimi tossed up and down in rhythmic motion, jerking from the potholes that the city fat cats failed to repair. She marveled at the majestic Catholic churches, garnished inside with carved pews, statues of saints, and red velvet kneeling pads, now frayed from the elderly that had confessed their sins and prayed for forgiveness. She passed buildings that had been granite banks and had anchored and dignified Detroit's city blocks but were now graffitied with day-glow paint and hillbillied into makeshift Holy Tabernacle houses of God.

Mimi questioned the choices made by the man she observed from her bus seat. He wore a tattered scarf around his turkey neck and rummaged through the garbage cans of trashed endeavors trying to salvage the thrown-out options like those he once had.

The salt encrustation on the bus's window made it hard for Mimi to study the nooks and crannies of a woman's face that pushed and fought her rusted shopping cart against the slush that lay frozen in piles along the street curbs. Mimi, being of cold nature herself, empathized with the woman as the biting wind painfully cut into her apple-doll face, making ambulation to the corner even more laborious.

As in times past, the old-timer found respite indoors while Polish neighbors shared camaraderie with each other, buying staples from the shelves containing stacked products both domestic and from their mother country. Mimi had read once that over seven million immigrants came to the United States from about 1880 to 1941. Mimi visualized the Rooskies wearing flour-dusted aprons and heavy nylon stockings rolled up just below the knees, gossiping as freshly-made pasta hung on wire racks beside buttered apple strudel that was waiting to be cut for dessert. The only preserves left from their old ways were the pungent brines lingering in the empty barrels that once contained pickled pig's feet and salted herring.

Mimi took out a crumpled piece of paper that she had placed inside her boot. It contained lyrics Max had written that best described how she felt about her trips downtown.

Twistin' avenues far as I can see,
Windshield wipers keepin' time

To a latenight mystery.
City streets got a fascination
I can't explain,
Tall buildings rise enough and a drizzly rain.

Fallen bricks and broken glass,
A hole where there was a door,
I'm looking into the lives of men from a world
that ain't no more.

What's happen-in here? I'm thinking to my mind,
Tires cross the old steel rail
Ghosts of the streetcar line.
Families and businesses, built with portal and
blood,
Washed away with what looks like
Some kind of biblical flood.

The reason for the ruin
Ya wonder what it was,
Everybody just gives a shrug and says:
"Well, just because."

Where are all the people?
The tulips and trash cans?
Made useless by a pale progress nobody
understands.

Where all our big fat cat
Civic leaders sittin' on high?
Sucklin' themselves at the public tit
While whole neighborhoods go dry.

Children in the doorways
The skinny arms that reach
The moon goes down, the sun comes up
A politician gives another speech.

Everybody's shoutin'
The town needs something new
Mebbe a couple of gambling joints
With a river view.
Alotta of grand ideas
Are just a passing wind,
Like ol' newspapers blowing down the street
Here we go again.

Take a minute to take a look
At what's left to save, if old Cadillac ever did come
back
He'd go right back in his grave.
  I seen a man make a stand
On the hood of an old Ford,
He held a bible in his hands
Yellin' "Praise the Lord!"

Shouting salvation in the dirt is
A gift for those
Livin' in a town where the banks are churches
And the churches all been closed.

I'll bet up in heaven no angel ever looked so cute,
With spit-shined shoes and a fine Holmberg
And a lime-green walkin' suit.

Interrupted by the view, Mimi looked out the bus window at the abandoned houses and weeded lots decaying next to Woodmere Cemetery where she knew her grandfather also rotted. Row by row the headstones etched the final quotations of everlasting life from the many immigrants who died against their will, not from fear of dying, but from their art for living in their new country, America. Mimi's Russian grandmother came to mind. She thought about her setting sail penniless on a ship bound for Canada that ended up in Michigan, later owning a twenty-five acre farm that she exchanged for her city house in the industrial area of Detroit called Delray. She perished later in a house fire where only the handle of her purse survived—perhaps an appropriate symbol after she scrimped and saved enough money to send her five children to college.

After a time the bus pulled up to Fourth Street and Michigan Avenue, the closest stop to Plum Street. The area was intended to be Detroit's art community center, blessed by Detroit's city mayor, Jerry Cavanaugh, but ended up with two or perhaps three art co-ops and a few head shops that sold counterculture paraphernalia.

Not eager to make the same mistake at the Climax Boutique, Mimi decided to visit the store that would be the safest, "Cabbages and Kings," because it had the most customers. She wanted to make sure there would be an escape route nearby when she talked to the shop owners. They happened to be as colorful as the candles they sold.

The tarot cards that were kept behind the counter held a special fascination for Mimi. The fortune-telling cards were extremely graphic, depicting the devil with jagged horns on top of his head, drooling evil spit over his prey of maidens. The doomsday card frightened her the most, but, ironically, it was the first card she inspected. Holding the card above her closed eyes she imagined what it would be like to know her future.

"Bad vibes," she shivered as she laid it down.

While shopping on Plum Street, Mimi purchased a tiny red seed that had an ivory stopper on top. When one opened the seed, twelve white elephants the size of pinheads spilled forth from their pomegranate-seed home. She could not wait to show Max her new prized possession.

With her purchase tightly secured in her mitten, she walked a mile toward the Detroit River.

"I remember shivering in the cold, planning on the bus route I would take to get home on. I also remember, while I was reading the engraved lettering *Salvation Army* on the top front, two-story building, feeling guilty of the lie I would tell my parents when they asked me where I had been all day. I felt a strong empowerment changing me, making me giddy with happiness. My childhood collided head-on with my newly felt independence, removing a stale-like feeling that wasn't doing anyone good and replacing it with a deep inhalation of Downtown's energies. I then inhaled a compelling desire and the need for action so I could start playing on this new playground."

As she entered the building, she noticed the Salvation Army's wooden polished floors and the racks of clothing that were on display. Even though the institution freely gave away used clothing to those in need, her mother's remarks were not so generous, chastising her daughter for bringing home old clothes.

"Get those cancer germs out of the house," demanded her mom.

But how could Mimi resist wearing the fine silks of a flapper dress or the tight curl of a Persian lamb coat when they could change her manner to fit a magical mood with hints of flirtatious but innocent behavior behind their rhinestone buttons?

Old Belgian lace wedding dresses hung sadly, the gaiety gone out of their long ago celebrations, pleading to Mimi's sentimental disposition. Feathered hats, deathly still plumes drooping from their continuous bowing and tilting—possibly caused by the Rev. C. L. Franklin's New Bethel Baptist Church—now lay silently in state singing to Mimi in Aretha Franklin's gospel style, "Hallelujah! Amen! Sister, rescue me, you have been saved!"

Body odor, stale perfume, and mothball chemicals reeked from the wool stitching that trapped the scent of past baptisms and funerals, continuing to play havoc with Mimi's imagination.

She eventually returned home with the packages from this bounty hidden from her mother's inquisitive eyes. With the bathroom door locked, she made a makeshift tent over the vent with her damp Maxi Skirt, as she waited for the thermostat to kick the furnace on. And when it did, a blast of hot air filled her skirt like a balloon, soothing her chaffed legs from the three-mile hike home from the bus stop.

Mimi did not want to get off the floor when she was summoned to dinner. She was too busy feeling happy and free.

CHAPTER THREE

"Ain't Nothin but a Maybe"
Rufus

Max and Mimi discovered each other's bodies at Ford Field, a secluded park circled with numerous pine trees and a sought-after place that stirred sexual desires Mimi hoped to pressure cook into reality.

In the beginning the couple met in a decrepit brick building near the Rouge River that contained a rest room for the park's patrons. A little old man, whose job was keeping the ancient stalls and sinks cleaned, was there every day. His walk was almost as slow as his talk. His only companions were a lanky grouchy man, with whom he played checkers, and a transistor radio he kept in his shirt pocket with the earphone constantly plugged into his ear.

It was on bleak winter days, the park's baseball fields hibernating under the snows, and the drooping pines standing guard, when Mimi and Max would meet inside the unheated pavilion. The caretaker, locked inside his space-heated room and usually taking his nap, provided the two with privacy. The muffled whistle of Henry Ford's museum train was blanketed under the low-lying snow clouds of Greenfield Village, making the train sound more lonesome than it usually sounded on its frozen tracks. Max and Mimi watched the pale afternoon light filter through the diamond-leaded windows and embraced in each other's arms. The snow shower falling outside dampened the soggy, moss-laden brick pathway, but was unable to chill the two hearts that were warmed by their inner bonding.

"At other times, we would regularly visit a street front, turn-of-the-century brick apartment building on Michigan Avenue that provided us with a spectacular view of Dearborn's main street. It also had an outdated but ever-so-quaint iron caged elevator door that we discovered while checking out the architecture. At the top floor lay a moth-eaten oriental runner that ran the length of the corridor. I never once saw anyone come or go from these rooms. But I did imagine that these tenants entered life's dreams initially expecting an exciting run to the finish line in the attempt to find out what life had to offer but faltered and settled for this apartment's safe haven security instead. Most people, I think, choose to remain in a comfort zone, reading from their armchairs and behind closed doors the volumes of books written about daring souls that gambled and flirted with adventures, instead of facing possible failure trying to experience it themselves. I imagined them blowing the dust off the mildewed pages that accumulated from their boring everyday routines. Those routines produced the same outcomes I desperately wanted to avoid myself."

At the end of the hallway sat a red geranium on the windowsill with an aura of Monet's lighting behind it. The filtered light reflected tiny dust particles that floated aimlessly, carried by random drafts.

The cast iron steam radiator sang a clanking tune of hisses and whistles while the water gurgling through the pipes acted like backup singers harmonizing and breaking the otherwise crypt-like silence.

It was the hallway of this building and the ratty pavilion at Ford Field that set the scene for Max to cast his spell, sprinkling onto Mimi's mind the dust of crystal knowledge that he loved her.

"He kissed me.
Sensual,
Unhurried and
Complete."

"The physical contact of Max's lips, and his bold, and yet gentle touch, triggered a tingling sensation within me. I did not want to run from the sensation. In spite of my innocence, I gladly volunteered and succumbed to the temptation of submission. He was protective of my vulnerability. I felt I could let my walls down because he never rushed me into anything that I did not want to try. I felt I was always in control. Thinking back I wondered whether Max's seduction of me was the patient, skillful quality of a player or that of an experienced lover, sensitive and sweet. But in any event, it was a time when my body responded to my mind's decision that I no longer wanted to be a virgin. I was seventeen years old and thought my decision would lead to a fairytale ending…and they lived happily ever after.

"My first sexual experience was a letdown. I thought the ritual of lovemaking was a step into an unknown land that would unlock all the mysteries of human desires corralled within the boundaries of intimacy. After giving my virginity away to Max, I thought it was understood that I was his only. Time would reveal I was not. Instead after a few tears that welled in my eyes, caused by guilt instilled by the teaching I had received from the Catholic Church and the moderate pain I had received from the act, I didn't feel any closer to Max than I had already felt. The physical part made me feel like I was being used because, unlike before, I expected a promise of commitment. But in its immediate impact, it was the before and afterward of the act that made me feel like a natural woman, which was what I desired.

"Max never just did it. He handled me like a porcelain figurine that could shatter if I was positioned incorrectly. He touched my skin like he was caressing the softest Victorian velvets. He smelled my hair like it was the finest silk from a Turkish bazaar, underneath a jasmine-scented twilight. I was totally naked on his romantic stage, my soul connected to his, stripped of all its earthly nonsense, seduced with a magical power of his kisses and taken for a ride on a magic carpet. Even though his lovemaking was physical, it was the emotional feeling of acceptance, the feeling of liberation that I craved."

⚭

The Summer of Love started when school let out for Mimi, nixing her alibi previously used to see Max on a regular basis. Her parents started to cross-examine her with questions about her summer plans.

"You are not gallivanting around the streets of Detroit by yourself. Those protest rallies attract drugs and hippies. Birds of a feather flock together. Can't you think of doing something constructive with your time?" Mimi's mother asked.

Mimi thought that protesting the Vietnam War was constructive. But to give peace with her Mom a chance, she got a summer job. Max surprised Mimi a couple of weeks later when he showed up at the Hudson Budget Store Grill where she had started to work as a counter girl.

"How did you find me?"

"I have my ways," Max answered with a loving grin.

He leaned over to give Mimi a hug. "Mmm, your hair smells like French fries," he joked.

Mimi's break times with Max were spent feeling summer charms warming her entire senses, again.

"My time with Max was spent mostly having fun. When I smelled a flower with him, I shared the thrill of simplicity. The cushion of cool moss beneath our feet became the sensation of intense tranquility. The warmth of the fading summer light became the rebirth of a dying day. The stream that babbled its pure drinking water quenched both our thirsts with its evanescent moment. We were in love, which caused everyday moments to become Zen-like in quality. Unlike all my other dates, he did not take me to events that would entertain me. He was the entertainment."

Mimi recalled one such evening when Max parked his car beside a hill on Hines Drive, overlooking a summer vista where Mimi could watch the weeping willow branches dance gently back and forth.

"Max drove a 1962 Mercury station wagon with a rearview window that was controlled by a push button knob on the dash board. After he parked Max opened the windows wide so we could hear the summer sounds that floated in. The crickets started their evening chirping, a lonesome and enchanting sound. We would watch the orioles flit to the side of the cattails. We were always talking about something, often laughing at our imperfections. If the conversation slowed, we would just sit and blend with nature and relish the smells of a newly-mown grass or listen to the bull frogs croaking in baritone."

Mimi continued, "There was a cardboard box in the back of the station wagon where Max kept his toys. The carton contained an oversized spark plug that was probably a store prop, a plastic Jesus that was stolen from a nativity manger, an assortment of ragged antique children's books, and a hodgepodge of trashed trinkets that captured his creativity. These items were used in various ways as props in the Lenny Bruce bits that he recited."

"Are you really a deep sea diver?" Max recited.

"No, schmuck. I'm drowning."

"With the corn stalks as his audience and the crows playing the critics, Max would stand alone as the sun gave way to the horizon. With hands upright to the sky, his enthusiasm and originality incinerated my inner dullness as he recited his own poetry. We validated each other's creative responses in a way that codependent junkies would have done, as the intoxicating love that we both shared ran through our veins."

Their favorite meeting place was beside the fireplace at the Dearborn Public library, in the Children's Room, which was on the second floor. The fireplace mantel had handmade inlaid tiles depicting detailed graphics of nursery rhymes that made it ever so charming. It was here, at a secret table behind the stacks, that Max showed the vintage cartoons that would later become the foundation of the Max and Mimi comics that he created for her.

Summer ended, senior year began, and Mimi's friends started to talk about going to Colorado after graduation.

"Towards the end of my senior year, I was smuggling Tom Rush and Hank Williams records into my French lab instead of listening to Sister Lacomb's *Parlez-vous Francais* exercises. The albums spun the traveling minstrel's stories of riding in open box cars, thumbing to the Navaho Indian's wide open landscapes, and sleeping under the stars in tent cities. I wanted to be a fugitive from my past, so I created a future, imagining myself, Indian-like, catching tumble weeds, living on the road in Kerouac-style, and being parched from the sands of the Death Valley deserts while I choked up the universal peyote-inspired answers about the Colorado-high of the Rockies."

The idea of living out west was appealing to Mimi. But her parents insisted that she attend college. Mimi's dad wisely stated, "You can be a bum, Mimi, if you want, but you are going to be an educated one."

"I knew what I wanted more than anything else and that was to be with Max. But he never discussed practical matters, let alone information about his past, and never worried about the future. As for me, there was...

No plan,
No commitment,
No opinion from Max about what I should do.
I left for college."

CHAPTER FOUR

"Born To Run"
Bruce Springsteen

Tears welled up in Mimi's eyes when she waved good-bye to her parents from the upstairs dorm room at Western Michigan University in Kalamazoo. The tears soon subsided and were replaced by anticipation of what it was going to be like participating in the first coed dorm in campus history. To Mimi's disappointment, her roommate was not a boy, but a farm girl from the heartland of the U.S. of A.

"She was hardworking, disciplined, a decent church-going girl—everything I was trying to run away from. I wanted to explore my Doris Duke attitude, which consisted of going to the places that I wasn't allowed to visit because of my conservative background. At the same time that my roommate was asking me where to hang the paper-Mache flowers in our room, I was smoking dope, checking out topless joints, and partying off campus."

Like the Indian dress Mimi tried on at the Climax Boutique with the chaotic colors of thread and the tiny reflective mirrors stitched on its loose fabric, so too was the nature of her new friends.

"My hours were not spent waiting for the library doors to open but listening to the revolutionary views for peace being discussed behind the doors of closed coffee houses. We were brainstorming ideas in social change, playing records by the Stones, and planning the next demonstration about what we could protest. The dope I was smoking was changing my perspective on things. But it was really the people's energy that was making my head spin. I was meeting famous 60's icons at some of the happenings, people like Peter Yarrow and Joan Baez."

Even though her new friends and places were distracting Mimi, she was still lonely for Max. Max was writing to Mimi, sometimes several letters in one day. The letters came to her in large yellow envelopes, spilling onto her lap as she opened them.

"Those were the days that Bell Telephone had you by the balls if you were sporting a long-distance relationship without much money for extras. There was no such thing as instant e-mail gratification or

Blackberries. We wrote letters instead. Max would send me poems, drawings, puzzles, and songs that he wrote.

"I'm the white line on the road you go,
I wind and turn, it's true.
The sun it colors me black in heart,
And the moon just finds me blue.
I'm good for nothing and bad for something, so slow,
I just, last and last.
But time and I are such good friends.
And good friends don't go fast."

It was unusual when several weeks went by and nothing came from Max since this last poem. Then finally a note arrived, postmarked Denver, which confirmed all along that what Mimi hoped in her heart was true.

"Gawwwd, what's he doing there?" She tore open the envelope and started to cry. "This can't be happening, what made him change his mind? I can't believe him. There is no way this could be!"

But it was true. Max took a trip out west lasting for two or so weeks and on his return he decided to be with Mimi in Kalamazoo.

Kalamazoo had a section of town that was the low-rent district called the Student Ghetto. This was the shabby chic area that was popular with the kids that wanted to live off campus. Oak and elm trees lined the streets and contributed to the naming of them, with outdoor potted plants adorning the numerous screened-in porches. Bikes locked to picket fences that had peeling paint, dogs running free, and a leather shop on the corner were all part of the appeal.

"The first week Max arrived we looked for a room to rent in the student ghetto so he could stash his guitar, his well-worn copy of *Dharma Bums*, and another pair of jeans that remained inside his backpack, along with a few other belongings he had taken to Colorado. We read in the *Western Gazette* newspaper about a small cheap room available, so we walked over to check it out since we weren't sure whether Max could live with me in my dorm room without getting in trouble."

"Oh you must be the ones that called about the room," the fiftyish, jovial lady said as she answered the door. She threw her head back and began snorting horse sounds as she bobbed her head up and down to the rhythm of her own laughter. She had yellowish buckteeth that were too large to fit inside her mouth, emphasizing the spit that sprayed from her words.

"She led us up four flights of stairs, talking nonstop about the downhill spiral of kids these days. The questions she asked us answered the background information she needed about our characters. Of course we told her what she needed to hear in order to rent the room from her."

She asked, "Are you both students?"

"Yes," Max lied.

She smiled when she verified that Mimi did not believe in premarital sex.

"You don't do drugs, do you?" she asked us both.

"Of course not," we answered emphatically in unison.

"We finally made it up to the cupola on the top floor. One had to open a trap door at the top of the stairs to actually enter the room of the widow's walk. The room's walls were floor-to-ceiling windows, six over six panes, which looked over the treetops ablaze with orange and red colors that the fall season had painted. It was breathtaking!

"Max laid his full month's rent down that very moment and the deal was sealed with a horsey snort from the landlady.

"We never set foot in the place again except to move his stuff out one month later."

❧

"I like you a lot Mimi, but I'm moving across the Valley to another dorm," stated Mimi's dorm mate. "If my parents ever found out about your dog living with us, let alone Max, well, they would never forgive me. I can't let them down. I hope you understand."

"I did understand my roommate's concern, but I also knew that the school would not let me live off campus the first year. And since Max was staying every waking hour in my room, I had optimistically hoped that nobody would say anything. However paranoia has a way of filtering into your psyche the way pot smoke seeps through unnoticed cracks underneath your door. So I was naturally concerned after one of my morning classes when I noticed an entourage of authoritarian officials stepping out of my dorm room into the hallway."

"What in the hell is going on?" Mimi asked, once inside the room, as she adjusted a picture of a monkey that Max had named D.B. Cooper that hung on our wall.

A blonde girl who was closing the door behind Mimi started to disrobe.

"Without answering my question she asked one of her own."

"Are you Mimi? I'm Mary, your new roommate," she said as she shifted her wad of blue bubble gum from side to side.

"The girl confidently swung my only clean towel, which Max and I were saving, over her naked body and proceeded to take a shower. The room did not look like she had moved in except that the bunk bed mattress was lying on the floor instead of resting on the bed frame."

"Oh, by the way, Mimi," she yelled from the shower stall, "I'm not really going to be living here. My boyfriend, Nevette, and I will be crashing at his pad from now on. So, if my parents call, front for me, OK? Make up something, anything, just don't tell them the real score. I can't believe you just missed him. I get so frickin' mad at him; I want to kill him at times! He can be a real fucker face when it comes to dealing with the police. I thought the pigs were real cool though when they tried to get my feet untangled from the bunk bed frame. Can you imagine what those paramedics thought we were doing with my legs straight up in the air like that? I could tell there was some snickering going on but still they were cool to act so professional."

"I wondered where Max was as Mary continued with her story."

"Nevette split when I started to scream, 'it hurts, it hurts.' As soon as he realized the yelling was due to my entanglement and not my climatic coming, he just totally freaked out!"

She continued as she stepped out of the shower. "He told me to shut up, and that's when I started to cry. He just ran out and left me there! I guess he dialed 911 down the street because the rescue knock came fifteen to twenty minutes later. I didn't know getting cobb could be so dramatic."

"I told her that it could. I shared with her the story about the time Max puked all over me while doing it at an old girlfriend's place we were visiting after eating a hot dog in Greenwich Village."

"What do you say, do you want to go with Mary Jo and me and find some cobb tonight?"

Mimi refused the invitation but instead placed a gentle kiss upon Mary's cheek, sealing her good fortune with her new future absentee roommate. Mimi knew now that the illegal living arrangements of Max and her dog, MoFo, would be safe.

And they were safe, up until the time gossip blew into the housemother's ears the following week. The housemother, Norma, a dyke, was an alternative-type of person herself who closed her eyes at first, ignoring most of the rules that Max and Mimi were breaking.

"If it wasn't for her, we would have been thrown out a long time before we actually were."

"Everything in Norma's world was taken to the extreme. Her makeup was a Barnum and Bailey's format with oversized, red lips and enough mascara on her eyelids to win first place in a Tammy Baker contest. Five pounds of jewelry dangled from her neck and, to top off her ensemble, her signature scent was *Jean Nantes*, which she poured over her body to cover up the fact that she had not taken a bath for a month.

"At times she was the most laidback person. But if she happened to be in a manic phase her screams echoed with the highest pitch and were accompanied with snarling hisses. This led to her vindictive behavior.

"Max and I wanted to get on the right side of the moon with Norma. The housemother suggested to Max and me that we should enter a Halloween door contest. This was to allow the other students to see how non-threatening we were by having us participate in their wholesome dorm activities. It sounded like a good idea since both of us loved Halloween above all other holidays, and we both liked to paint."

Hieronymus Bosch was Max and Mimi's favorite painter so they decided to pay tribute to him by painting their own *Garden of Delights*. Their masterpiece would have all the same types of ghouls that you would find under your bed at the midnight hour. The eerie figures had snakelike bodies and rat heads. Eggshells cracked open, releasing Beelzebubs that escaped by flight, flying towards the laughing moon with Norma's face painted on it.

Alongside the blood-drenched rivers, perched on the deadwood of snarling-faced trees, vultures with butts for heads and penises for noses created havoc for saints that were painted ironically above the vultures.

Even St. John flung his velvet-clothed body over the opened-legged naked maidens of the underworld. There were ostrich-size eggs hatching out every kind of sexual act, depicted by frogs and cockroaches. Vampires of the night glided down to the towers of mankind with their leather bat wings. The closing scene was of charcoal doves roosting on dungeon gates' finials that lanced their rotting prey into the chaotic atmosphere.

The Halloween door contest backfired on Norma's plan to diffuse the dissimilarities that the students had for this artistic duo.

Mimi explains, "It only displayed how we were like oil and they were like water, and that we would never be able to mix in a world where people could not think outside the box without being afraid. Because we did not paint jack-o-lantern faces with smiling grins and the traditional black dressed witch, and because we paid tribute to an artist we liked that they regarded as deranged, we became more like their enemy.

The painting amplified the black mark inscribed by the general student body consensus. They concluded that our condemned souls, along with those of our friends, the midnight tokers and a few night crawlers, would be smoldering in the ashes of Hiroshima, lying in state among the worms entombed in the Christian cata-combs of Rome, and forever destined to wail along with the paid mourners at Mussolini's gravesite, summoning the devil himself who concurred with them that we were both condemned to go to hell! The students, furthermore, concluded that Max and I cared not about the law and order that everyone else was obeying in the Valley of the Dorms."

"But the thing that actually broke the monkey's back was the day we brought Hezekiah home. He was a squirrel monkey whose beady eyes reflected the desire to escape the confines of his caged world. He needed a loving home so we smuggled him into our dorm room."

Hezekiah was a tiny creature that chirped like an exotic jungle bird—not like you would think a primate would sound. His arms were golden, dripping with a honey color that melted soft yellow pigment into the rest of his coffee-brown fur garment. The Zorro-like mask of his face, sporting a theatrical smirk, lanced Max and Mimi's hearts with an endearing jab.

"The first moment we brought him home, we immediately opened his birdcage cell. He sprang into action, grabbing an apple that was lying on the counter. The carnival thief was wild with excitement, imitating a masked bandit from the storybook past. He gallantly jumped on the back of his majestic steed, MoFo our dog, and paraded around the room."

Afterward pandemonium broke out when MoFo tried to get Hezekiah off his back.

"Lamps fell over, crashing light bulbs onto the floor. Dirty dishes that hadn't been washed since we began living there smashed into glass pieces. Unread schoolbooks still covered in bubble wrap and the university's pamphlet on rules and regulations became confetti, ripped into shreds from their previous Havisham situations, thrown by the monkey's paw at the dog. The curtains substituted for Hezekiah's trapeze as he swung from curtain rod to table and bed."

With all the loud commotion taking place, a violent knock came at the door. In entered Norma in a manic mood herself. Max and Mimi had been busted!

"That does it!" she screamed.

"I tried to reason and give you guys a chance. I ignored the constant complaints from the other students. I blocked my ears with my pillow to all your Jim Morrison albums and my nose to the never-ending aroma of smoke. I even tried to keep an open mind when your weirdo friends would prop the downstairs door open after-hours when they were supposed to be locked. I can't take it anymore.

"It was even rumored that the two of you were involved in all those floating pumpkins on the Valley's pond!"

While Norma kept ranting, Mimi recalled how Max and she had planned, with the precision of an English-jewel heist, the prank that the housemother was referring to. Both of them went to great lengths not to be seen carrying thirty pumpkins up three flights of stairs after stealing them from a nearby farm. While they were washing off the pumpkin's field dirt in the dorm's shower, the drain became clogged, filling the hallway with water. They hurried, mopping it up before anybody could see them.

Norma screamed on, "The campus police had an aggravating time and the university received a reprimand from the Audubon Society!"

Now Mimi became exasperated, "What about us? Think how hard it was carving and lighting thirty jack-o-lanterns incognito while the mean geese were hissing their orange beaks and flapping their feathers trying to defend their eggs on their floating nest island. We had a hell of a time!"

Mimi's hands were now on her waist showing her annoyance with Norma. She asked, "Don't we get any recognition for making the pond gorgeous for Halloween?"

"Oh you're going to get recognition all right, Mimi. First I'm going to report that you were the ones who created that entire fiasco, and then I'm spilling the beans on you about Max, your dog, and that monkey living here." And she did all that, but not before Hezzy leaped onto Norma's back, defending his mistress. Norma began to spin around the room. Around and around they both went. Norma was trying to grab Hezzy's tail when he managed to get tangled up in her hair as he frantically tried to get himself free. She left madder than a hornet and with a monkey on her back.

The following day, Max returned from a morning walk only to find Mimi crying into an open letter. It was official. The Board of Housing demanded that Mimi get rid of her animals, man and beast, immediately, under code 99895467, or receive disciplinary action that could result in expulsion from Western.

With the monkey nestled in her lap, MoFo warming her feet, and Max's sympathetic arms around her, Mimi sighed, "I guess this means they want us to move."

CHAPTER FIVE

"Were You There?"
Johnny Cash

"This book is taking longer to write than I anticipated. It is the therapy I need in order to forgive Max
and give the hurt I experienced closure. He indeed
required forgiving, even though I know now I could
not have had a long-term relationship with him
because he was incapable of being faithful. Regrets
in living become wisdom in dying. But still the
cherry picked memories within sublime recall emerge
when I'm longing the dead to arise, resurrecting the
euphoric feelings one had for their first love. Is it the
unresolved issues I still feel buried alive that causes
me to challenge my comfort zone now? Maybe I...

Remember to forget,
Remember to regret,
Remember to create?"

"Tonight it is raining a special rain. I call these evenings, *Long Black Veil Nights*. That's the time when the soft drizzle is gently tapping against my windowpane and the whistling wind moans unanswered questions while begging to be answered for life's review. The Moroccan lanterns flicker their diffused glow against my bedroom wall like a vintage reel-to-reel projector's light creating and casting forms in the shapes that perhaps represent my shadowed past.

Squares for imprisonment,
Circles that surround self worthlessness,
And triangles with all sides of love felt."

"An atmosphere for remembering the mistakes I have made and forgiving the ones that were made against me."

The phantoms that project on Mimi's wooden screen continue to ask, "Mimi, Mimi, what have you done to deserve love's rejection? You who are so arrogant with your calculated decisions and thought processes, a friendly little element that makes life's challenges seem so easy. You, who have learned now, have made sure that all who love you could never be allowed to leave your personal equation without shattering your devotion and gratitude.

"And yet even with this self-examining, confident proclamation, Max's desertion still haunts you. With the stage set, Mimi, let your memory stir up your constitution to remember the day you moved into your new apartment, thirty-one years ago in 1973…"

⚜

"Baby, I have already explained, I got to go back to Detroit. I can't move in with you at Mt. Whitney I got to take this job at Ford's. It has nothing to do with you personally."

"Isn't it ironic that the casual 'live in the moment' attitude that I admired in Max in the beginning of the relationship turns out to be the one that tangles me up in the end? I had never intentionally hurt anyone before. But then again, I also never took the time to find out if I had. Was this the case for him? Some of us were guilty of 'What's in it for me attitude' in our days of youth. But because I was blind with love, naïve, or perhaps cowardly, I did not challenge Max's move back to the motor city. But I did secretly question his motives."

> Female roommate wanted
> Close to East Campus
> Own bedroom, $150 a month
> Share utilities; call
> Susie, 6886473

It was from a bulletin board at Kroger's that Mimi noticed the ad. And after meeting with Susie, she hastily made the decision to take the apartment in spite of what her friends told her about the personality of her future roommate. She could no longer go back to dorm life. She needed to act fast. The university only gave Mimi a two-week notice to vacate. She now could legally live off campus.

Susie had a prosthetic arm after losing the use of the limb to polio ten years earlier. Motorized so the fingers could move, the device fitted in a special holder that she religiously plugged in each night, recharging her rubber appendage and making her life more bearable.

It wasn't the contracted and distorted way the upper arm limply fell, dangling at her side when she wasn't wearing her device, or the better than thou attitude that Susie displayed during Mimi's interview that made Mimi feel uncomfortable. But she became wary hearing what her friend Betty Jo said about Susie afterwards.

"I know how Susie really is. Rommel used to live with her. She is a control freak. She is absolutely hateful, Mimi! Nobody can stand living with her."

"Nobody wants to live with my fur babies either," Mimi said, remembering the dorm and all the *No Pets* apartment ads there were. "Besides, I need help with my expenses. Mealy worms are expensive and you know how Hezekiah loves to eat them. I have dog food to buy not to mention the stray cat I feed and the birds in the park. I do what I have to do! Susie said she didn't mind my animals." Mimi placed her hands on her hips to make a point.

Unbeknownst to Mimi, Susie needed a roommate as badly as Mimi did because of her own expenses, and she realized it would be easy to manipulate the laid-back Mimi. Susie thought she could tolerate her animals until the lease ran out, and she moved.

As Mimi was signing the lease and wondering if Hezzy was going to chew on the rubber arm, Susie was already applying for a position in New York.

"I was not happy with my new living arrangements. I mostly just stayed in my room with my pets and waited for when Max would come on the weekend. After a couple of weeks, I was getting more and more lonely during the nights, so I decided to give my time away to people who wanted it.

"Wayside West was typical blue collars joint with a juke box playin', a pool table bumpin' and the guys a pinchin'. I worked in extremely short, velvet hot pants, serving beer and Sing-a-pore slings to the local rednecks of Kalamazoo. The song, "You're so Vain" was popular with the after-work, go-get-drunk crowd. I hated the song then like I still do now. It wasn't a good place to work 'cause the boss was trying to hit on me. "Every night after I had wiped down the countertops stinking of sour beer, I took out the trash cans that were overflowing with smelly cigarette butts left by men that were just as smelly. I was exhausted from the whole scene. I knew I had made the right decision to stay in school. My dad was right about education. It gave people more options—even though it was difficult to attend early morning classes and still clear my schedule for Max. I was lonely for him and wanted to feel special. I understood perfectly how Hezzy felt the first time I let him down when I forgot to bring his special, nightly cocktail cherry home one night.

"Myuk, Myuk, Myuk," his endearing voice came from behind his blanket-covered cage, letting me know he was waiting up for me after a late night Saturday shift. Hezekiah's golden arm turned upwards from his cage and then wound its way out, finding the crack to receive his anticipated Pavlovian treat. I had miserably forgotten his cherry delight.

"Myuk, Myuk, Myuk,' he chirped. His gentle calls changing to jungle squawks when he realized his disappointment in me. He started to rattle his caged bars when he noticed that I had forgotten his long-awaited dessert. I tried to appease him by opening his cage door, setting him free so he could choose from the other fruit I had put out, but he only wanted his cherry. It was when I noticed a tiny teardrop trickling down the side of his masked face that my own tears began to fall. Together we discovered we did not feel special anymore—the way love was supposed to make us feel."

As the weeks carried on, Mimi covered up her disappointment by laying underneath the blankets with Max on those weekends he managed to visit. She never let on her doubts about his stated intentions for moving away—he had said he just really needed a job.

The Wayside's male customers pointed out to Mimi that Max was having his cake and eating too. She would rather leave the frosting on his future visits than take into consideration the possibility her cake may be getting stale. By denying the possibility she might be just being used, she could keep the treasured past locked away unscathed.

"It was better to have less than nothing at all." This heartfelt deduction Mimi would soon learn wasn't true.

Mimi especially loved the walks together with Max that usually started on the dead-end street where the houses sat close together, shivering off their coats of paint, and where the garbage cans lined the driveways like garden ornaments of the ghetto.

At the end of the cul-de-sac stood a house that had an oversized aquarium inside that was anchored, stage center, in the front of a picture window. From outside that window Max and Mimi would watch the fish tank's underwater world. The blue-tinged, rippled water and the tropical fish darting around pink coral displayed a quirky contrast to the dirty encrusted snow under Max's and Mimi's boots. Mimi meditated with thoughts, superimposed by her reflection on the fish bowl's glass, mirroring the questions...

"Cold or warm?
Swim or sink?
Cosmic dust or earth's student?"

As they walked along on one chilly afternoon, the randomly smudged mosaic handprints embedded on the window made by the ruffians who lived inside these walls complimented Mimi's Zen questions.

Max carried a pocket-size tape recorder, dubbed, "TR" with him a lot of the times. It was on this occasion he captured a candid moment with one of the rascals in the back alley that made this walk more memorable.

The kids were using brooms for sticks since they did not have the luxury of any store-bought sports gear. Two milk jugs filled with sand stood as a makeshift goal waiting for the hooligans to smack a barbecue charcoal puck into its scoring space.

Max singled out the oldest-looking boy for the interview. He and Mimi noticed holes in the boy's boots, but he appeared unconcerned with the wet cold slush that was seeping in. From time to time, the boy would use his tattered sleeve for a handkerchief, while "TR" recorded the background squeals every time the other children scored a goal. The smacking of the brooms and a distant horn blowing played like an intro for an NPR human-interest story called *The Good Old Days*.

Max began the interview with, "What's your name?" The young rascal was not in the least intimidated, so Max recorded the boy's ten-second response to his opportunity for fame.

"Troy," was his reply.

Without any further ado and with no other comments, Troy's voluntary, newsworthy, and earth-shattering update was announced with a Kentucky drawl into TR's mike.

"My sister peeses the bed!"

Then he ran back into the crowd to continue his play in the already in-progress hockey game.

For a young woman like Mimi who loved spontaneous moments, Max provided the sugar coating for everyday happenings such as these. It was part of his charisma that he could walk by the front doors of a neighborhood church on any otherwise uneventful day and without hesitation share in the experience of a Pentecostal religious ceremony, making their day special.

She used to love the rituals of her own religion, Mimi remembered, until the Catholic Church changed its tradition in order to make it more appealing for the changing times. It was during the early '60s that the Vatican thought it would be wise to update the Latin Mass to English and play guitar music instead of the mournful Gregorian chants.

Mimi did not care for the change into "New Age" in which the churchgoers hung up felt banners on plastic poles with flower powering, witty quotations. It cheapened the sacred ceremony. She much preferred praying in front of gothic, martyred saints with their dripping wax tears while she listened to the tolling of the bells, dinging and donging amidst fallen angels that had mortal sins staining their souls. Kumbayah tunes were not her thing.

She followed Max and MoFo to the back pew during the in-progress service at the Pentecostal church on a Sunday morning walk. MoFo immediately sat on the cement floor preferring to block out the loud, vibrant gospel singing with his paws covering his ears.

Unlike the Methodist and Catholic churches in the area that had elaborate stained glass windows that sparkled like Ethiopian jewels, this church had only one single pane of glass on the north side of its front-door panel and a green one on the south side. Mismatched chairs presented themselves as pews. There were only two pictures that adorned the sanctuary walls, one of baby Jesus sitting next to a rock and one of Mary with a painfully bleeding heart, dripping its contents into a puddle of blood.

The music coming from the congregation made up tenfold what the church lacked in silver and gold. With Max's tape recorder running, he was able to record the church members stomping and clapping with Holy Roller enthusiasm that could rock the ancient stones off the tower of Babel. As the choir sang out, Mimi's heart opened again in the belief that Max's love was genuine and he was her amazing grace. It still would take some spiritual work for her to realize the authenticity for loving anyone would depend on loving oneself first.

"Praise the Lord," Mimi prayed aloud, looking over to Max as he returned a quirky smile.

Her enthusiasm was short lived. Max cancelled their next weekend together just as they were leaving the building. Mimi found herself back in church a week later trying to pray out the feeling of being let down.

Again, Max called and told her he couldn't make it the following weekend.

"Hiya, baby," Max greeted her over the phone. "I'm sorry, but I just can't come over next Saturday or Sunday. I have a chance to put some overtime in and, Christ sake, you know I could use the money."

Guilt,
doubt or
truth?

"I'll call when I can get near a phone. You will be fine without me."

He hung up the phone rather abruptly and left her wondering why he did not want to talk further. What was the cause of the obvious change in his mannerisms towards her? She had an uneasy feeling and decided to go back to a Catholic church so she could try once again to recapture love's blessings and confess her past sins.

"It couldn't hurt," she decided.

"Bless me Father for I have sinned. My last confession was about four years ago. I stole a brick of Colby cheese from the corner store, so I think God might be punishing me," she confessed while thinking about Max's indifference to her.

"Are you sorry?" whispered the priest through the screened window.

"Yes, very."

"Will you steal again, my child?"

"Yes," she said as her stomach rumbled from hunger. She wanted to answer truthfully and not add lies to her lists of sins.

"Then I cannot forgive you."

"I am sorry," pleaded Mimi, "but I'm also hungry. It seems that I never have enough money left over at the end of the month because my animals have to eat too. MoFo eats like a horse and then I have this new kitty cat, DaDa. The pound was going to put her to sleep if someone wasn't going to adopt her the next day. They were planning to kill her. So you see, I just had to take her home."

Mimi was getting increasingly agitated thinking about the warden euthanizing DaDa. "My monkey needs special bugs called mealy worms for his protein requirement. You must forgive me!" Her hands went from a folded position to her hips.

"You are aware that the Catholic Church does not condone stealing even if it was for a just cause?"

"I'm sorry if the Church thinks it is so wrong. But I do what I have to do. And besides you are getting paid to forgive me, aren't you?" She stormed out of the confessional not waiting for an answer.

"I don't need no stinkin' priest to forgive me, I'll forgive myself," she defiantly told herself as she returned home and slammed her bedroom door behind her.

She wanted to shut out Max's indifference and she wanted the priest to forgive her weaknesses. She cried about God's unanswered guidance. Tears came down as she started to face the reality that her life wasn't charmed anymore. When she heard the knock at her bedroom door she answered it like a sniffling little girl who had been bad.

"What is it, Susie?"

"Please Mimi; do you think you could keep the noise down for once? Tomorrow is extremely important for me. I'm having a dinner party for some future clients. Remember, I told you about the company that I want to start-up, educating the handicap about the special aid and laws they can use to their advantage? Well these people I'm inviting to dinner have the finances for such a business. They are coming to listen to my pitch. I'm begging you, please don't screw it up. Make sure you keep the monkey away, the dog and cats locked up, and your music quiet. Please, Mimi, this means a lot to me."

Susie had realized for some time she was fed up with the circus sounds that emerged from Mimi's bedroom on the weekends when Max visited. The various moans, chirps, and orgasmic yells that came from the mouths of human and beast made it impossible for Susie to conduct a normal life. Her new business venture was a genuine chance for her to move on and improve her life.

"Not only will I keep the noise down for you Susie, but I will even help you clean the apartment," Mimi answered, aiming to please and feel appreciated.

When Mimi volunteered her cleaning services she did not know she would also be scrubbing her present living arrangements away, too.

"I'll do a good job. You wait and see, she told Susie"

"I polished every surface in the kitchen for her. I even scrubbed the floor, thinking it would be an appropriate penance for stealing the cheese. Before I went to bed, I turned the lights off and unplugged all the appliances."

Mimi woke to the promise of a new day. While she lay in bed, even though her eyes were still groggy, she tried to focus on all her familiar surroundings, making her hopeful that all was right with the universe. Hezekiah was jumping around in his cage, eating a leftover banana. DaDa and MoFo slept in blissful unison at the foot of the bed. Birds chirped and darted around the outside bird feeder that she had hung up the previous week. Mimi felt satisfied knowing she helped Susie instead of focusing all her attention on Max.

It was the calm before the storm. The harmonic moment was broken by screams coming from the kitchen. Susie's contorted face erased the blissful, serene aura lingering in Mimi's room and replaced it with an outrageously loud yell.

"I had a chance. A decent, honest-to-goodness opportunity to start up a new company and get out of this hellhole!"

Innocently Mimi asked, "What have I done?"

"I can't stand it any longer. I live in a godforsaken zoo." Susie fell to her knees when Hezzy tiptoed towards her and started to stroke Susie's hair to comfort her, sensing she was upset.

"You just had to ruin it for me, didn't you?"

"Please, Susie, tell me what I have done?" pleaded Mimi.

"You are nothing more than a spoiled little bitch! I can't wait to move out of here. You depend on everyone. You are more handicapped than I am. You use your sorry-ass man to validate your artwork, and yet he alone monitors how cool it is. Your pets are proclaimed free, but are they really, Mimi, when they are chained with the burden of entertaining you?

"You smoke dope and drink in order to avoid the reality how pathetic you are inside. All you want, you say, is peace, tranquility, and harmony. Ha, what a joke! Peace does not mean having sex all day and night, and lying in bed 'till two o'clock in the afternoon. Tranquility does not conjure up images of smoking your brains out then flicking the finger in retaliation at the people you have screwed over, intentionally or not. And as far as harmony goes, well, that doesn't mean unplugging my arm the night before, sabotaging all the things I needed to do today. That is what your random act of kindness did for me, unintentional or not. You have unplugged my arm! Thanks to you, I can't cook dinner…it will be impossible to type my resume. I can't even wash my hair, you miserable jerk.

"I had a thousand and one things to do today. How do you suppose I can do them with one blasted arm? Perhaps I can get an hour out of it by recharging it now. At least I can pick up some carryout. What a pain you are. I hate you. Rooming with you was the biggest mistake I ever made. Job or no new job, I'm out of here."

Mimi ran frantically from the room. She fell on the bed and began to sob the most heart-wrenching cry while her MoFo licked the salty tears that fell down her cheek.

"I just want to be loved. I'm so sorry Susie. I didn't mean to. What with Max ditching me this weekend, I just wasn't thinking. I thought I was unplugging the toaster, not your arm. I have been so lonely. I don't know why it is, but every time I try to give all I can, I end up hurting others. Please forgive me. I'm so sorry, Susie."

"I wanted to make it up to her and I had every intention to do so. I was crying on the bed, thinking up ways I could make amends. I needed comfort, so I cried out for Hezekiah who always provided me with unconditional love."

"Where are you Hezzy?" She heard a cheery chirp from the closet. "Where are you, my furry man? Come here," she commanded.

When he didn't come, she dragged herself off the bed and headed toward the closet where he was hiding.

"Hezzy, come here, I feel awful. Come pet me."

Mimi opened the closet door. To her shock she found her jungle beast in the corner chewing on Susie's arm with one of the fingers gnawed off the base of the rubber hand.

"Oh no," Mimi wailed in horror. "Now Susie will never forgive me."

With her hands covering her face, she went back to bed and started to cry all over again.

CHAPTER SIX

"Daddy Was a Rolling Stone"
Temptations

By the time Max came up the following weekend, Susie had already moved out. Mimi was beside herself because Max hadn't called since the ordeal with Suzie and he was never home when she tried to reach him. She was unable to tell him what had happen until he arrived.

"And then I found Hezekiah hiding in the corner of our closet, real quiet-like, nibbling on poor Susie's rubber finger," she told him.

With her lips pouting and her voice quivering, she continued, "Half of the finger was hanging from the corner of his mouth. He was using the tip as a tooth-pick. And that's when I lost it, Max."

"For Christ sake, Mimi, I know it wasn't intentional. But it seems like lately you manage to get into one kind of crisis or another. Jesus, what are you going to do now for money?"

"Well you did say you were working overtime. Maybe you can help me out," Mimi said with an impish grin. She was feeling safer now that Max was near.

"Mimi, I know this probably ain't the best time, and I don't want to hurt you, but there is something I got to tell ya."

Puzzled, she looked up. "What is it?"

Mimi had never anticipated the breakup coming let alone the speed in which it happened.

"Instantly his words started to unravel our history and already dog-eared the past days I had spent with him. From Lessons in Love 101, Max's carefree attitude was a textbook example of just that, carefree. Looking back it was to my advantage the breakup occurred. His ambition in life—except for the pursuit for a good time emphasized by his temporary friends and art projects—was totally absent. He had no tolerance for anything that made his life uncomfortable or required responsibility, such as a mortgage or kids. His were not qualities that were ingredients for a long-lasting relationship. It would not have cost my dignity, though, if I had only known then what I have since learned. This, of course, was my karma. I can now see that my first love was the last affair I would have that would be based on my assumptions that it would work out rather than being grounded in the reality of the man. I was only wishing for what it could be instead seeing what it was."

"Don't you love me anymore?" a teary-eyed Mimi asked Max.

"Please stop crying. I can't answer your *whys*, Mimi. I just can't fucking see you anymore. Jeez, people break up every day."

"He then heartlessly added salt to my open wound by demanding that it would be best if Hezzy go with him until I was settled with a new roommate."

In shock, Mimi mutely watched as Max placed Hezekiah in the hallway. The confused little monkey chirped his final good-byes to his mistress as the chamber door shut between them.

The verdict had been announced.

"See ya, Mimi!"

Poof! Just like that they were both gone.

No warning,
No crime and
no comfort.

"Max never explained why he left me so abruptly. In a song he wrote and sang to me thirty-five years later in the halls of a ruined church he sang,

"If my woman wants to know the truth,
Don't tell her any lies.
Say that the girl I was kissin must have had me
hypnotized.
Hell it was that low cut blouse, that must have
made me go blind.
Tell her I went away, with a friend of a friend of
mine."

"At the time, I thought Max was cruel to cold
turkey me at the end of our relationship like that.
Inhumane or not, I now think it was the best thing he
could have done. Unexpected change at worst can be
the best challenge. And this reality immediately took
hold of me.

"That afternoon and the days that followed, I
grabbed for a bottle of rye whiskey. I needed the sweet-
ness of the liquor to dull my senses, so I wouldn't feel
the pain of desertion. The stark reality is that I felt
my soul's preservation was severely damaged by Max's
departure. I asked the question "what went wrong?" and
took another shot, fell back asleep, asked the unanswera-
ble question again, drank, and slept, repeating the cycle.

"My hangover shattered my dreams. The reality of
never seeing him again came back up at the start of
each new morning. I would get sick, as if throwing up
my dependence on him. .

"But as fictional as it sounds and while my heart continued breaking over the question as to why, I pulled myself back together after three long days and three longer nights. Still, I had to pull sad minutes into hours and then hours into days.

"Mercifully it was a clean break. I was not given the luxury of believing in the false hope that there was the slightest chance we would get back together. Max gave me no mixed signals. I stood naked as I was."

Do you remember the young Mimi who wanted to scratch out the blackboard values that she questioned because she felt stifled from the old ideas of the establishment and wanted to feel life's rawness? She now felt vulnerable and exposed to a world that seemed to hold no values. Miserable with Suzie gone and almost no money, Mimi moved out of the apartment.

She decided to move temporarily into the Howard Hanger House. Her friend Rommel lived there, but would be away on a music gig in Florida for a couple of weeks. Besides she had no other place to go.

Bumming a ride out of Kalamazoo brought no thrills as it did in her freewheeling high school days. The ride left her stranded along the shores of Lake Huron, feeling quite concerned because she still had another mile and a half to go.

"I'm glad you're not here, Hezzy. I miss you terribly," she told herself, "but I know how you hate the cold."

And cold she was. The thin shawl she was wearing did not give sufficient protection from the lake's chilly wind that blew off the frigid Canadian shores. Mimi kicked the heavy, corrugated box that held her impractical belongings to the side of the road. But as she did so, a sharp rock cut the twine holding the box together in half, spilling the only possessions she had in the world onto the ground.

"Damn, damn, damn," she mumbled, fearing the Japanese tea service that her Uncle John had given her from his travels as a merchant marine had broken. Mimi was pleased when she inspected the eggshell china cup in the dim sunlight that managed to show itself occasionally through the clouds. She appreciated the beauty of the oriental lady's profile embedded inside the cup's bottom, which was silhouetted by the sunlight passing through it. The fragile vessel survived so many years, defying the odds of being broken while constantly being used by others.

"It would have been a sin if it ended up broken. If broken would the slivers of glass make me bleed?" she asked herself.

Interrupted by a roaring car engine that was fast approaching, she looked up annoyed and saw a young college-age man behind the wheel of an MG.

"Need a lift?"

Without waiting for an answer, he got out of the car, stumbling over Mimi's open suitcase as he tried to pick up the items scattered all over the ground.

"My name is Russ. Let me help you." He snickered approvingly as he held up Mimi's feather boa and threadbare silk nightgown.

Already annoyed with him from his preppy sports car and his bold acts, she grabbed her garments away from this too obtuse intruder.

Placing her hands on her hips, Mimi defiantly said, "No thanks. I can walk the rest of the way myself."

Russ looked around and realized just how far she was from anywhere. He was concerned for her safety.

"But you're shivering."

He was irritatingly right. She was too cold to refuse his second offer for the ride. After a few tries, Mimi finally put her things back in the broken suitcase and got in his car.

Russ grabbed a wool lap blanket from the boot to wrap around her shoulders. Mimi was grateful for this kind gesture and presented him with a tiny smile—a rare occurrence in those days.

The car tires crunched over the frozen gravel as it sped off. Mimi felt liberated from the miles behind her, but only until he turned onto the grounds of an old estate where she was intending to stay.

Guarding the entrance was a decapitated Diana-the-Huntress statue, whose cemented torso continued clutching a bow and arrow with her iron fist that hung peacefully from the body. The old stone goddess was damaged. But her foundation still remained strong.

The MG stopped at the impressive, columned doors of the once exquisite home of the pharmaceutical family, the Upjohn's. The romantic ruins were still livable, although time and decay had taken their toll.

"I'm late," Russ informed her, shaking her tiny hand and feeling sorry for her without quite knowing why. "I have to go."

Though not wanting to leave her there at the doorstep alone, Russ had no other choice than to say goodbye to her. As he did, he could not help thinking that she was like a baby bird that had fallen from its nest, meekly waiting to be eaten by a river cat.

"Good-bye, you beautiful frightened creature, you," he thought to himself.

From the silence that settled in after Russ's car zoomed off, it seemed obvious that nobody was home at the communal mansion. It left Mimi feeling cold as stone. She gazed at the toppled statue again, took a deep breath, shivered, and went inside through the unlocked front door.

"I don't want to see anyone, anyhow," she lied to herself. "I'm so drained, all I want to do is take a nap," she thought as she noticed the shabby couch in the front parlor and felt the house's oppressive tomb-like vibe.

Her velvet shawls made ideal bedding, covering the holes in the couch's upholstery. As she climbed underneath the covers, she wiggled her cold legs together feeling the soothing scratchiness of the bits of gravel that had fallen from her skirt's hem. With her eyes drooping she began to imagine what Max might be doing at this exact moment.

Rain had started; causing drops from the mansion's decayed water-damaged plaster to begin plopping in pools onto the parquet floorboards, competing with Mimi's tears that started to fall as well. Her barely audible crying gave way to heart wrenching sobs as she continued to dwell on her loss. Then suddenly her tears stopped when she realized that the pillow she was crying into smelled of mouse droppings. It was then she heard the voice of her old roommate, Mary, coming from the front door.

"Mimi, Mimi, you made it! I want to hear all about you and Max splitting up. I'm going to pour us both a huge glass of Merlot. Did you know he wanted to get some cobb from me the night you floated all those god-damn pumpkins on Hadley's pond?"

An appalled look came over Mimi's face caused by both the stinking pillow and the news of Max's failed attempt to get Mary's amour. After an hour, Mary poured out the last of the wine, holding up her glass to offer a slurred toast to Mimi's courage.

"To Mimi and how well she is handling the breakup from the fucker face, Max, and all his cheating ways."

Mimi clinked her goblet against Mary's glass. Mary was totally unaware of the depth of Mimi's despair over losing Max.

"Mimi, you are so strong!"

It wasn't out of bravery that Mimi made the decision not to try to right Max's wrong by condemning him. She simply had no other options. Secretly she longed to hear the phone ring, again connecting her back to Max. She was capable of forgiving him even now and continuing on like nothing had happened just as long as she could resume reading the funny papers and laughing again with him. But instead she replaced the longing with the desire to kick the face of the moon in, smash its beams against one another so it would hurt like she did.

Her weakness retreated into a space that would keep her safe from her true feelings of despair and loneliness. For now she gathered the broken pieces of her moonbeam that continued glowing with love and warmth, and gingerly placed them into the trashcan, believing that she could still get them out in time should Max return. With that thought in mind, she started the next day hung-over with the hope of finding a new job.

CHAPTER SEVEN

"Running on Empty"
Jackson Browne

A new store opened across town that had a novel marketing strategy for middle-class Americans. That store was called Kmart. Their goal was selling quality goods at discount prices and changing the customer's ideology to a self-service mindset.

There was a time when giants like Hudson's Department Store had the expensive, mechanical elf window displays during Christmas time and the magical wonderlands that covered entire floors. But now they no longer had the sales figures to justify its expense.

The shopping experience that Hudson's created in its 1940s heyday was legendary, but started to dwindle by the late '60s. During its day the exquisite mahogany display cases held Spanish leather gloves or gold cigarette cases. White-gloved elevator ladies, who announced what items could be found on each floor, were rapidly being eliminated. Customers wanted to save a buck, and the store had to cut costs. Civility was being replaced by lower prices in the corporate, American eyes. Free home deliveries, back to school extravaganzas, hand-painted murals that adorned the chandeliered dining rooms of these mercantile institutions were now gasping their last civilized breaths. It seemed that no longer in Mimi's lifetime would she be able to experience such customer service.

Mimi's mannerisms and grooming still followed a regime of faded elegance as existed in her soon-to-be outdated Hudson's. Her gypsy mannerisms and the basement-style clothing did not correlate well with the progressive corporate-world image. She was a living oxymoron.

Mimi was educated, earning her Bachelor of Business Administration in management in less than two years. But her vocabulary failed to show her potential when she used words like *ain't*. She would feel at ease with her prim and proper Gamma Phi Beta sorority girls at an afternoon tea and then swear as well as any sailor could at a local dive. She continued to set her table with chipped-rimmed Baccarat crystal while she hid her bare feet underneath lace tablecloths that were hand embroidered by Belgian nuns. Mimi nibbled on Swiss chocolate, only to find herself short on cash for dog food or rent. So it is of little wonder that she decided to start working for the bargain-hunters store, Kmart, at the same time that her beloved department store doorman was closing Hudson's for the final time.

The Kmart seasonal merchandise was laid out for Easter, displaying the stuffed bunnies and the crayon color wicker baskets on the day Mimi applied for a customer service position. Moments before her interview, she mischievously entertained herself by poking her fingers through the yellow, marshmallow candy chicks inside the pink cellophane wrapping. She hated the taste of these sickening sweet, confection birds. She still thought it was perfectly appropriate to continue with this destructive ritual, which she first performed when she was a little girl.

Mimi thought Max would have been amused by the way the department heads pushed around a cart with a tacky blue light on top of a five foot pole, marking the spot where the pre-selected sales merchandise was to be found. The blue light spun and twirled as the manager blurted on his foghorn.

"Attention, Kmart shoppers! Men's underwear briefs marked down from $4.99 to just $2.99! Just $2.99, in an assortment of colors, too."

After the announcement there would be what sounded like a stampede of horses racing their way to the underwear aisle, under the twirling blue light. All that for a measly two-buck savings! The blue light special made people feel like they were not overspending. It was a kind of second coming for the bargain hunters while they herded themselves over to the markdowns.

The Kmart return policy was nothing short of a miracle unto itself. The store would take back anything, at any time, no matter how long ago the item had been purchased as long as one had the receipt. It was Mimi's job to make sure the customer was satisfied.

"Can I help you?" Mimi asked an elderly lady that brought in a mysterious looking paper sack. "Do you have a receipt?"

"Yes, yes, I have a receipt, dearie." The gracious lady gave Mimi a sweet smile as Mimi pulled from her bag what felt like was a stuffed animal that the lady had perhaps purchased for her grandchild. To Mimi's horror it wasn't a toy at all, but a dead parakeet that she had bought two days before.

"I didn't know this bird was so nervous when I bought it," the elderly woman explained. "The foolish bird broke its neck while Daisy, that's my cat, dearie, was playing hide and seek with it. I would very much like to exchange it for another bird. One, should I say, who isn't so skittish?"

Mimi handed back $5.95 with a Kmart-return-policy smile after she explained to Mrs. Bates that the store just finished a sale on birds and they would not be getting any more in for a long time. Mimi suggested that she should try a stuffed bird filled with catnip instead and assured her that Daisy would find it quite satisfactory.

Clyde was another amusing customer. He was from the South, and figured out he could get a brand new pair of cowboy boots every three to four weeks by exchanging them for another pair he had just returned if he kept his receipt. He paid no mind to the fact that the boots were just getting broken in. A deal was a deal, regardless of the blisters that made him limp out of the store.

Cowman Charlie however was Mimi's favorite regular. He would bring back bags of half-eaten food and later claim some kind of bug was in the remaining half.

"Mimi, I bought this here bag of potato chips two days ago and what do you suppose was found in the bag? A cockroach! Do you know what is worse than a cockroach?" He answered himself by slapping Mimi on the shoulder, "A half of a roach!"

Cowman Charlie's story changed only with a different kind of half insect found in the bag.

"Chin, chung," sounded the cash register.

"I'll see ya in a couple of days," said C.M. Charlie.

"Watch what you bite into," warned Mimi.

Mimi began working twelve-hour days, staying busy, keeping her mind off Max. Her working behavior helped glue her paper-thin state of mind into a workable solution, getting her through the daytime hours. However at sundown her fortitude sank with the sun.

Marissa, a former college friend, started to live with Mimi after Max broke up with her. "She had been working at Kmart and we were living in a two bedroom apartment on the top floor of a rundown house in back of the Mt. Whitney apartment building. We shared a communal toilet with the downstairs tenants, but we had a private bathtub in the kitchen. We placed plywood on top of the tub, so we could use it for our kitchen table as well. The only thing going for the dump was that it was cheap, and, as I remember, it had a rather large window facing west that made way for some spectacular sunsets. It became a party house and crash pad. I had a bunch of kittens that kept the place smelling rank. Mimi's dogs had the run of the place as well.

"We would go to this basement bar called the Rathskeller just about every night. It was walking distance from the house. A corner of the bar was reserved for the chess players. Dimly lit lights hung down over the pool tables, casting a haze of cigarette smoke that settled in the basement. Now Mimi could shoot eight ball better than any hustler that challenged her. Her dad taught her when she was quite young on their family pool table. In fact our rent, a lot of times, would come from the winnings she earned playing. She would wear shawls of lace that draped loosely about her. They revealed a full view of her cleavage when she took a shot. Now that I think back, maybe it wasn't her good shooting that attracted the guys, but the revealing view—none of us wore bras in those days.

"We both had long hair and the skinny, you know, flowers-in-your-hair kind of look. So it was real easy to pick up these cats. Mimi was always putting down the drunks, even though in reality, she was the Queen of the High Ball Court."

Mimi sadly reflects about that time, "I started to self-destruct in spite of my noble efforts. I wanted to get as far away from myself as I could. The liquor I was drinking and the scumbags I was bringing home cushioned my confidence, a thing I hid behind my bad behavior. The truth of the matter was that regardless of what I could have done or not done in the relationship with Max, it would not have mattered in the least. It had nothing to do with us here, but it had everything to do with the chapters of destiny that we charted for ourselves in a different space and time. But I lacked this insight. I continued to sustain my desperate feelings that fermented in a cesspool of hopelessness, temporarily refreshed by cherished past memories, but always ending up in a state of self-doubt."

Marissa added, "Mimi would bring home the most disgusting men from the Rathskeller. I recall one particular night she came out of her bedroom with black markings all over her face, arms, and neck."

"What in the hell is all over your body, Mimi?"

"I don't know. What are you talking about? You're scaring me!"

"Go look in the mirror. You'll see what I mean."

It didn't take long until Marissa heard Mimi's screams, "Yuck, yuck, oh yuck! How disgusting! Gawd! Get it off. Get it off!"

"It was moustache wax smeared on her breast and face and everyplace where his lips had landed on her," said Marissa. After this discovery she told me the incident was the first pothole on a road to regret.

"The next incident was a deeper hole. Mimi staggered home from the bar as usual bringing with her a guy named Dick. He wanted to fix Mimi a Mexican fajita dinner. I thought to myself, maybe this cat will be different from the others. Mimi had way too much to drink because she chose to sleep it off rather than to eat Dick's dinner. The next thing I heard was Dick screaming at the top of his lungs that his penis was on fire."

"Oh my, Jesus, God! It's stinging like the devil. Holy shit! It hurts! It's burning, godammit! Get some ice, fuck. Mimi, do something. Wake up and help me!"

Mimi explained what happened the next morning. "Dick literally took matters in his own hands after dinner when he crawled into bed with me. I was too drunk to wake up to his advances. He didn't realize he still had jalapeño pepper juice on his hands from when he chopped the vegetables for dinner. When his self-pleasing rub started, he was unaware of the painful consequences that would make him the hottest man in town."

"With the constant commotion in the house," Marissa continued, "it was hard to live a relatively normal life. But what finally convinced me to move out was the time Mimi brought home three drunks, making living there now dangerous. Fortunately, Russ had been in Mimi's shadow this whole time, sort of acting as a protective friend. He had picked her up hitchhiking to the Howard Hanger House a couple of months before and since he had been hanging around, keeping an eye on her. It was not an easy job, I might add. He was desperately in love with her."

Marissa continued with the memory, "I opened the door for the drunken entourage because Mimi, as usual, had forgotten her key. The sight of her was alarming. Mimi's black mascara was running down both her cheeks from the rain. She wore a wet feather boa that was draped around her neck and looked like a dead animal.

Her wide-brim vintage hat was lopsided on her head and ripped fishnet stockings completed her disheveled ensemble. Her left hand was holding an empty bottle of whiskey, while her right hand was tightly wrapped around a piece of sisal twine tied to the neck of yet another rescued puppy. She found this one whimpering behind the trashcan in the bar's alleyway. I heard Mimi mumble that she knew how the dog felt being dumped.

"My pity for her turned to anger just as one of the drunks puked all over our floor while the puppy squatted and then managed to produce a puddle of loose shit. Shortly afterward the sober, protective Russ threw the first punch at the drunk who tried to forcibly kiss Mimi and accidentally stepped on the dog's tail at the same time.

"Mimi was her own worst enemy. She had a big heart when it came to rescuing strays in a pickle, and that included humans and animals. But she should have been concentrating on saving herself. Many times I would see her get frustrated and then sad while she placed her hands on her hips, sighing, and whispering Max's name. I don't think she ever got over losing him.

"The last I heard about Russ was that he moved out west alone, and had a job planting pine tree saplings. Mimi eventually moved to North Carolina and had his baby. How the four strong winds do blow."

CHAPTER EIGHT

"You're Lost Little Girl"

Jim Morrison

The party was over for Mimi. Two months had passed. She no longer heard the clinking of ice cubes in the scotch tumblers that melted with the sun's glow, heralding the accountability of a new day.

In exchange for her sanity, she allowed herself to be out of character, living on the square. She stopped drinking and started to date Russ. Russ proved a safe but dull haven for her. As hard as this was for Mimi, she made an effort not to pine away for Max, providing a temporary respite to allow Russ's love. The Band-Aid over Mimi's deep wound came off when she made the decision to call it quits.

She did not love Russ even though he couldn't have been kinder. He was very sweet and protective of her.

Time had made her feel stronger. It was not fair to him to continue, since Mimi believed she could never feel anything for him other than gratitude. After she told him how she felt, he tumbled out west alone, all dried up from Mimi's unrequited love.

Mimi continued to be optimistic when Christmas season came along. She was lonely at times, but was soothed and comforted by listening to music and taking fresh winter walks with MoFo. She learned again to enjoy being alone instead of with a man. The time she spent thinking under the branches of the dark sleeping trees helped her emerge with a plan for building a different life without Max. She was successfully healing from her destructive mood. Like the Diana statue relying on its foundation to be upright, Mimi believed that her solid upbringing and reliance on God for forgiveness was to become the basis for her survival.

Weeks passed. Mimi decided to get Hezekiah back and then move south. A move to a different climate might help wake her from the hibernation she was in.

To keep up her positive but fragile momentum, she took another sip of herbal tea and spoke softly to MoFo.

"Today is going to be different. I'm going to change my way of thinking. I'm going to start by making this dreary room cheerful instead of depressing."

She opened the drapes just as the sun miraculously followed her cue, its rays breaking through the leaden skies. She hugged MoFo and told him that a Christmas tree would look spectacular in front of the window, making her typical gesture with her arms on her hips to emphasize the decision.

The afternoon held promise. Mimi's anticipation remained bright along with the sunshine. She did not know that the day's events would become a pivotal turning point away from her belief that Max's rejection was due to her inadequacies. The negativity she felt toward herself and that held her captive would soon vanish. Empowered by positive energy, she took command of her optimistic mood.

While she looked for her Christmas tree, she drove past the same fields where she and Max had stolen the pumpkins to place on Hadley Mill pond that long ago Halloween night.

She voiced her thoughts aloud. "MoFo, we are going to be happy by finding us the most beautiful tree. Why you ask? Because we deserve it. We are going to bring it back home, put shiny tinsel on it, bake gingerbread men, and string popcorn! We can even give some of the popcorn to the wild birds outside my bedroom window! Won't they like that? We can save a cookie for Hezzy too, so when we pick him up in a week or two, he might not be so cross with us for letting him go with Max. We will all be together again. All one big happy family."

A very loud ker-plunky sound broke Mimi's conversation about her future plans and replaced it with sudden apprehension. She pulled her Mustang over to investigate the sound. She did so even though she was scared of what she might discover. Venturing out from the warmth of her car, she found it was just a "bump in the road." While noticing the lonely bleak landscape, her dainty silk-slippered foot slipped into an icy pothole. .

"Gawwd, I got my foot all wet."

The wind started blowing from the north, changing direction from the south. She shivered and wrapped the scarf tighter around her neck. The sun was gone.

"Thank God, MoFo. All the tires look good. We must have hit the pothole I fell in."

After inspecting the tires, Mimi got up from bended knees and, with head held high, her eyes zeroed in on a pine tree about one hundred feet away. The tree was majestic and powerful. Its branches outstretched. She knew she had found her tree without any help from Max.

"MoFo, just look at that astounding tree. It is perfect for us."

Overwhelmed with the excitement of finding a special tree, she forgot about her wet foot and scrambled for her shovel in the backseat of the car. She wasn't actually going to kill the tree. She meant to dig it up and replant it later in the spring. But when she tried to dig, the shovel could not penetrate the frozen dirt. Mimi struggled on until her mitten hands slid from the shovel's handle and smacked MoFo in his muzzle. Frustrated by the lack of progress and desperately wanting to prevail, she decided to use her ax. Chop, chop, chop. The crisp thuds sounded as the ax struck the defenseless tree. With the final blow, the seeping pinesap that flowed out from the tree's veins was very noticeable. Mimi's nostrils dripped, overcome by the smell of the spicy scent. The sacrificial tree bled its stickiness onto Mimi's hands, finding its way to her eyes and stinging them as it blurred out her vision. The Xmas tree's uncooperative branches lashed and scratched her face as she clumsily tried to shove the tree into the backseat of her car. Her eyes continued to sting as she tried to rub out the pain that the sap was causing. Disoriented by the temporary blindness, she imagined she heard the tree wailing for human-like revenge.

"I'll get you for this."

Disturbed, horrified, and crying, Mimi drove off with the tree. She heard the tree's imaginary threats again, accusing her of killing it. This time she was unable to shrug it off. A peculiar dread descended over Mimi. Instantly she felt a heavy sin had been committed. She knew her vision was blurred from the sap but, as she looked around to find out where the voice was coming from, her suspicions were confirmed. There was a man in bib overalls running down the road after her car. The nasty remarks she heard were not coming from the Fraser fir, but rather from a farmer screaming and waving a pitchfork in the air.

"Come back, you little thief. Come back here. I'll get you for this! Hey what the hell are you doing chopping my son's tree down? Get off my property. Get off!"

"Our Father who art in heaven, hallowed be Thy name," Mimi recited from the Lord's Prayer as she tried to figure out what she had done to make the farmer so angry with her. "He has hundreds of pine trees, so why would one tiny tree make him sooooo mad?"

Abruptly her thoughts came to a standstill when one of her back tires did the same.

"Cha ca, chachoo, cha ca choo," revenged the tire.

"Oh no, now what?" she thought, as the distressed tire interrupted her getaway.

A slow leak had caused the tire to become nearly as flat as a pancake. Miraculously the car kept on truckin', thumpin' its way over the gravel road. Mimi continued to drive until, after a few miles, she found the car impossible to steer. She managed to maneuver to the side of the road and rolled down the window, waiting for the farmer to catch up and hit her over the head with his pitchfork. But instead of a violent assault, he never appeared. There was only the tree in the backseat, MoFo in the front, and the "caw" of a single mournful crow outside, warning his feathered friends about the impending weather.

Mimi thought, "How could things get any worse?"

As if she had asked the gods the question and they had responded, the unthreatening skies turned to a wintry mix of black and gray. The wind clashed with the oncoming front and unleashed frozen particles out of the accumulated pockets of vapor. As the snow intensified, it seemed like it was following a choreographically prepared orchestration directed by Mimi's tears. The more she cried, the more inches fell.

Yes it was true that she was a wounded little element, and her trusted devotion had been shattered. However she would soon come to realize that sadness in life is not produced by terrible things people have done to her, but by her allowing, and participating in, her own personal self-destruction. By numbing her pain with alcohol, drugs, and sex, Mimi had failed to gain the strength it takes to fight the truer injustice of losing self-confidence. Could she regain the love of herself that she deserved from the beginning?

Mimi cupped her ears with her hands, blocking out the accusatory moans of the wind.,

"Murderer, murderer."

"No, no, no, you don't understand. I'm the one who is dead! You, tree, glisten and sparkle for anyone who will adorn your short life in the season's festivities. It will be me that will see the bareness of the room after you've gone. It will be me who shall feel the emptiness when you are no longer there."

As the tears continued rolling down her cheeks, Mimi noticed dangling from the tree's branches, a metal dog tag. The inscription on it read, *Planted to commemorate the life of John Billings who died January 30, 1970. May his memory grow stronger with the life of this tree.*

She was overwhelmed by this discovery. Dazed and not knowing what to do next, she broke down and started to sing.

"All the lonely people, where do they all come from? All the lonely people, where do they all belong," she sang off-key while she failed to notice the tapping of icy snow pelting the car's window that shielded her.

No wonder the farmer was so mad at her. She started to cry again. As she looked for a tissue in the glove box, she found a metal flask beneath some smoking papers.

Wiping her nose on her sleeve, she took a big swig from the flask. After months of sobriety, the liquor burned as it trickled down her throat. Instantly it made her feel warmer. She took another sip and then a gulp, singing louder.

"It's coming on Christmas, they are cutting down trees, ohhhhhhh, how could I be so dumb? They're putting up reindeer and singing songs of joy and peace. Ohhhh, what's the matter with me," she asked herself after finishing the flask.

The storm outside her window had turned into a major weather event. Five inches had accumulated on the windshield alone. The drifts had made it impossible to navigate even if the car did not have a flat tire.

Mimi wiped a circle of fog from the window and, in her drunken haze, saw a ghostly vision of Max.

"Oh, you have come back!"

The ghostly disarray of motion swirled, jumping from tree branch to branch. Snap! Snap! After each break the vision would laugh uncontrollably, making Mimi annoyed with its shenanigans.

"Stop it. Stop it!"

The ghost metamorphosed into water, dripping with his coolness, then froze in a rough image of an iceman. It motioned with a frozen finger to Mimi, directing her to follow it into a dark tunnel.

"Oh no. I'm not going in there with you. I'm too warm inside my car to go follow you to where it is cold."

He continued backing into the cave, his shimmering sparkle blinding her eyes. She could feel the intense pull of his words.

"Come with me, come," he said, enticing her with his finger.

The last thing she heard herself say was, "Thank Gawwd, you don't exist anymore. Thank Gawwd that the reality of your betrayal does. I'm OK where I am, alone."

Afterward, finally admitting to herself how she felt, she fell into a deep sleep. The last thing she saw as she dozed off was Max's brittle finger shatter into a hundred pieces while his figure melted into a puddle.

CHAPTER NINE

"Second Story Window"

Marc Benno

The first sensation Mimi felt after waking from her life-altering change was the sharp bite of the whistling wind making its way through the cracks of her car. MoFo, acting like a fur blanket, kept Mimi from perishing from the frigid temperature outside. Still groggy, Mimi thought she heard a knock at the passenger side window and then a man's voice.

"Hey, you in there, Are you all right? Do ya know where you are?"

"I do very well remember where I should be," she lethargically responded to the question.

But unlike Juliet's death that tragically ended with a happy dagger, the end of the person that was Mimi at last came with the happy demise of her dependence on Max and acknowledgement of his heartless treatment toward her. Without further ado, Mimi's freewill became just that: the will to choose the memory of Max's love with gratitude and joy. His love had come at a time in her life when she needed him to develop who she was now. She did not have to compromise her integrity when she stopped denying that the breakup was caused by his betrayal and not her inadequacy. She now knew that up to that point, her memory of her time with him had been obscured. She had remembered only the good times but did not see clearly enough the inevitability or predestined end of the relationship. A haze was now lifted from Mimi.

Mimi recalled, "The same drive that compelled me to find my genuine identity by rebelling against my parents surfaced again from the split with Max. Only this time I had to find myself, alone, without his approval and guidance backing me up."

The guy at the car window, whose name was Jackson, said, "Open the door; we are going back to my place. If you don't know by now, there is a blizzard going on. You can call a tow truck from there."

"We drove up to his farmhouse, which was terribly rundown. It had tattered plastic sheets nailed to the window frames—a cheap way to keep in the heat. I was skeptical of the place right from the start. But what choice did I really have? At least it would be a dry place for MoFo and me. Then I could call for help, like he suggested. The only problem was I didn't have any friends to call."

Freezing at the front door while Jackson fumbled with the stuck doorknob, Mimi noticed a couple of aluminum pots scattered in the yard. One had solid ice in it. The other contained frozen cat food. The door finally opened and several cats ran in. "Get out of here, you motherfuckin' cats!" screamed Jackson.

Mimi's intuition told her that he was not as nice as she initially thought. Her guard was now up. Bowing for Mimi to enter, she hesitated and then cautiously stepped inside.

The room was filthy with dirty dishes stacked in the sink and dried spaghetti sauce stuck on large areas of the counter top. There was a cracked plastic, avocado-green lounge chair in front of an oil drum that had been made into a wood burning stove. Nearby an axe wedged itself into a tree trunk that doubled for a side table. On a nearby table, mold floated atop the lingering soda in a coke bottle.

He pushed his bed in front of the fire, motioning for Mimi to rest there. Guarded, she sat at the edge of the cot and tried not to touch or smell the pile of rancid rags that were his work clothes. She listened to him swear at the ashtray he had accidentally knocked over when he had moved the bed. MoFo lay protectively at her feet as any good watchdog would.

"You goddamn ashtray," he screamed, with hate in his eyes.

After a few minutes, Jackson left the room to get a beer. Still a little high off the alcohol herself, Mimi began to relax. The heat radiating off the embers started to thaw her cold feet and, with Jackson gone, her mind drifted to earlier, happier times: the Detroit bus rides, her first kiss from Max, the day they brought Hezekiah home. All the old memories made her smile, again.

"I'll make that call now, Jackson," Mimi said. Her eyes were still closed in a relaxed state of consciousness. She was feeling stronger and, to her amazement, not sad.

Jackson was standing in the living room's doorway, his arms stretched to the arched doorframe.

"I don't have no fuckin' phone," he said. "There is no one around for miles, you stupid bitch. Why don't we make the best of it?"

Tugging at his belt buckle, he said to himself, "I never fucked a hippie bitch before."

Mimi wished she could have been a romantic writer, ending her novel with a climax such as becoming blind while her Gothic mansion burned to the ground in front of the north Atlantic seas or maybe never as to be so cruel as to kill a mocking bird. But as it concluded, her story did not end with her becoming a victim again. Among the rat-infested nest of Jackson's tangled sheets and ragged cow manure-stained work clothes, Mimi took charge of her life once again.

The slap delivered across her face jarred her into survival mode. MoFo lunged after Jackson causing his second blow to miss as Mimi stumbled over the body of a seemingly dead cat while she reached for the front door. Mimi was just turning the knob when Jackson grabbed her shawl's fringe and threw her backwards. Mimi fought hard and managed to get to the front door for a second time. She wrenched it open only to slip on the icy front porch into the arms of a burly, but good-looking man with a gun. Miraculously instead of a tiresome customer like the one at the Climax Boutique who unintentionally saved her from the parasite, Nikki, this time it was the law itself!

"Why little lady where are you going in such a hurry?" the county Sheriff wanted to know.

"We had a call that there had been a Fraser fir tree stolen from the neighbor's farm and the description of the car matched the one a quarter mile or so down the road. Would that there car be yours?"

Mimi flew into the cop's arms, crying with relief, "Yes, yes it is! I take full responsibility for my actions," she said as she extended her wrists to be handcuffed.

"I don't think there is any need for that," the police officer grinned. "You and your dog get into the backseat, and we will sort this out at the station."

The police car dipped and slid its way down the country lane, leaving behind the harmful assault. Mimi cared enough about herself again to fight back. Mimi's authenticity and personal confidence, enabled by the fine values that she had learned from her parents, were glowing inside her like sparklers. It was like the confidence she felt when she first fell in love with Max. Mimi had learned to love herself again.

A now wiser Mimi listened to the murmur of the reassuring and safe engine that propelled her through the bleak landscape. The gnarled trees reminded her of the frozen iceman. The car bumped in the same deep potholes that had earlier brought her journey to a standstill. Then she noticed the ever hopeful, glistening green Christmas tree that was dying in the back seat of her car. None of these obstacles threatened her anymore. Instead she felt challenged in a purely positive way by her own spirit. She would forgive all the bad things people did to her. She would move into the present moment, good or bad, adjusting to all people and circumstances that presented themselves. This new way of thinking caused her doll-like eyes to be wide open as she anticipated an exciting new time of life without her Max.

CHAPTER TEN

"Flowers Never Bend With the Rainfall"
Simon and Garfunkel

Mimi felt butterflies in her stomach as she walked up to Max's bungalow duplex back in their hometown of Dearborn Heights. She knew he had been living with a girl that Pam, her old high school friend, said he had met in a bar around the same time he was going to see Mimi on the weekends. Mimi also had been told that she was very beautiful. But the news she really did not want to hear was that they fell head over heels for each other. So it was not surprising that she would feel apprehension as she walked up to the door.

Mimi had made plans to move out of the state and had already sent down the few belongings she wanted in North Carolina. Pam was also moving down there and suggested that she could start fresh. The moving van that Pam rented still had room for a few things. So when the opportunity came, Mimi packed her rocking chair, a crate full of record albums, some boxes of clothes and a few household items so that her stuff would be waiting for her when she reached North Carolina.

Mimi would be far away from home and pregnant. It appeared her birth control failed with Russ. She had been sick with a throat infection and the doctor put her on antibiotics, which apparently decreased the potency of the birth control pills she had been taking. That was one she had never heard before. After she found out she was going to have a baby, she wrote a letter to Russ. Knowing only that he was out west, she gave the letter to his brother to forward it. She knew letting Russ know about the baby was the right thing to do. She found out years later Russ never got the letter.

"For the cover-up at home, I told my parents that I had been accepted into the Kmart management training program in North Carolina. There was no way I was going to tell them that their good little Catholic daughter had gotten knocked up by someone she did not want to marry.

"I finally managed to tell them the truth about the baby thirty-five years later, thinking it would let my skeleton out of the closet. After I told my mother I had a baby out of wedlock, she responded by quoting the Bible, 'Mimi, you reap what you sow.'

"My father made three comments after listening to my story with a tear trickling down his cheek. He was very quiet as I told him my story. I had thought he might be distressed about what a disappointment I was. Instead my dear, loving father told me he wondered about the father of my baby, how sorry he was that he, himself, wasn't there to comfort me, and, with a gentle smile and a forgiving twinkle in his eye, he said he was glad I didn't tell him at the time because he did not think he would have been able to handle it.

"I thought North Carolina was a good place to hang out until I gave the baby up for adoption," Mimi continued with her story. "I had a guy friend that lived in Chapel Hill who told me I could crash at his place until I found a job. He lived in a log cabin, which appealed to my adventurous senses. I was sure that my decision to give up the child would hurt no one except me. I had decided the infant would have many more advantages than I was able to provide for it. I did want to keep the child, but I was just too fragile still. I did what was right for the baby. I did not hear from Russ. Since I was the one that got myself into this situation, I would be the one to get myself out. The only thing left to do was to pick up Hezekiah from Max and keep on moving on."

Mimi knocked softly on the front door. No answer. She picked a dead flower from the row that lined the walkway. She was on bended knee, facing away from the door when she heard it open. She turned around to see Max watching her. The thorn from the shriveled bush stuck her finger as she handed Max the single dried, dead rose.

"Thanks." He smiled after he took the rose and wiped the blood from her finger onto his jeans. He told her to come in.

As Mimi was sitting at the polished dining room table, she looked around the room and realized it was not a place she would expect Max to live. The furniture and vibes were sterile, middle class, and conservative. She noticed a canopy bed through the doorway. After commenting on it, Max told her that he had made it for "her."

Max stood over Mimi. He looked very sad. He asked her how she had been doing. Mimi looked into this stranger's eyes and politely answered, "Likewise, I'm sure."

Moments passed and she looked down, tears welling up as she realized there was no future to be drawn from the past.

Mimi cleared her throat and wiped her eyes. "Max, I've come to get Hezzy," she said. "I'm surprised I don't hear him." Her voice sounded upbeat, perking up at the mention of his name. "I'm moving to North Carolina. I'm leaving this very minute. I've got it all arranged. I even have a cherry and a cookie for him."

Mimi took out a tissue with red dye all over it. "See the sweater I knitted for him, too?" An assortment of miscellaneous trinkets fell from her pocket as she pulled out the sweater. "Remember how he hates to be cold?"

Her voice was getting more and more excited as she started to think about the monkey. She held up the tiny garment for Max to see.

"Where is my little man?" she said, smiling at the prospect of reuniting with her beloved pet. Mimi peered around the kitchen door, then looked inside the bathroom but came up empty handed.

"Where is he, Max?"

"Oh God, Mimi." Max put his hands in his face with a heart-wrenching sob.

"He is dead. Christ, he is dead! I'm sorry. I'm so sorry. I put him in the garage 'cause Rachael didn't want him in our bedroom. I was going to get him later, but we both fell asleep. It was extremely cold that night. Oh shit, Mimi. He froze to death. I forgot about him, and he goddamn froze to death."

Mimi put her arms around Max and tried to console him. The sweater she made for her little monkey slipped through her fingers onto the floor. No words needed to be said.

The northern wind was at Mimi's back when she left Max crying in the doorway. The wind pushed her away from his place with a forceful gust. Snowflakes dusted her tangled hair. Freezing at the curb, her thumb out, she quietly looked up at the leaden skies and told whoever was listening, "I really loved you, Max. I will always keep you and Hezekiah in my heart."

Mimi did what she was compelled to do—she headed south. A makeshift leash made from the fringe of her shawl kept MoFo from the dangers of the highway traffic. It was not a long time before a car stopped to pick them both up.

"Hop in," invited the driver, moving his Coast Guard uniform jacket to the back seat. "Where are you heading?"

Before answering, Mimi sighed as she looked out the car window at the withered wildflower stalks that had once dazzled passersby with their beauty when the sun's glow made their colors vivid. Mimi was confident that when the winter's stormy months passed, the chicory and Queen Anne's lace would once again take root and regain their strength, growing there or somewhere else alongside the road's pavement.

"I'm going where the sun can shine on my face, mister," she said, turning to MoFo and giving the dog a heartfelt hug. Smiling, she added, "We are both going to North Carolina."

The End

In loving memory to my monkey, Hezekiah